CRYPTO-CURRENCIES AND THE BLOCKCHAIN REVOLUTION

BITCOIN AND BEYOND

BRENDAN JANUARY

TWENTY-FIRST CENTURY BOOKS / MINNEAPOLIS

Twenty-First Century Books™
An imprint of Lerner Publishing Group, Inc.
241 First Avenue North
Minneapolis, MN 55401 USA

For reading levels and more information, look up this title at www.lernerbooks.com.

Main body text set in Futura Std
Typeface provided by Adobe Systems.

Library of Congress Cataloging-in-Publication Data

Names: January, Brendan, 1972– author.
Title: Cryptocurrencies and the blockchain revolution : Bitcoin and beyond / Brendan
    January.
Description: Minneapolis, MN : Twenty-First Century Books, [2021] | Includes
    bibliographical references and index. | Audience: Ages 13–19 | Audience: Grades
    10–12 | Summary: "When Bitcoin was first released in January 2009, each digital
    coin was worth only a few pennies. A single Bitcoin is now valued at over ten thousand
    dollars. This book examines digital cryptocurrency and the blockchain technology that
    makes them possible."— Provided by publisher.
Identifiers: LCCN 2019046569 (print) | LCCN 2019046570 (ebook) |
    ISBN 9781541578777 (Library Binding) | ISBN 9781728401591 (ebook)
Subjects: LCSH: Bitcoin—Juvenile literature. | Cryptocurrencies—Juvenile literature. |
    Blockchains (Databases)—Juvenile literature.
Classification: LCC HG1710 .J36 2021 (print) | LCC HG1710 (ebook) | DDC 332.4—
    dc23

LC record available at https://lccn.loc.gov/2019046569
LC ebook record available at https://lccn.loc.gov/2019046570

Manufactured in the United States of America
1-46980-47849-4/16/2020

TABLE OF CONTENTS

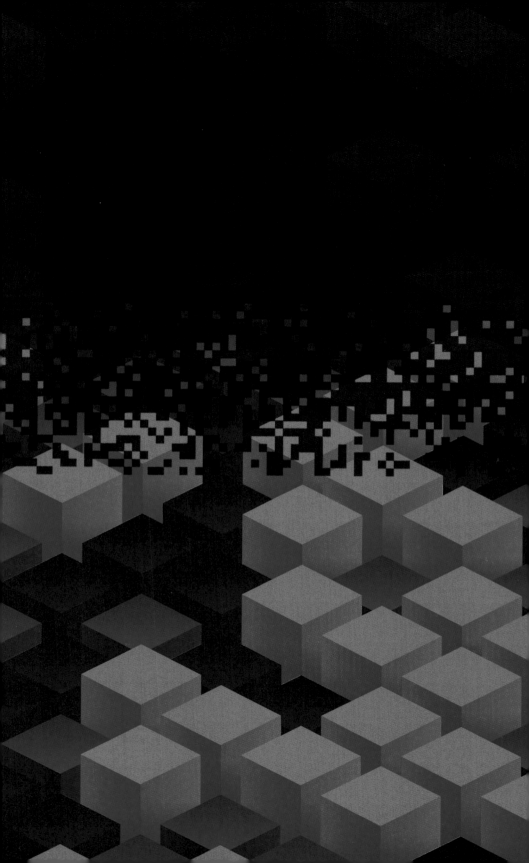

INTRODUCTION

In January 2009, a mysterious software developer known as Satoshi Nakamoto exchanged a specially designed file with another developer. The thirty thousand lines of code were a form of digital currency that Nakamoto had proposed several months earlier in a paper titled "Bitcoin: A Peer-to-Peer Electronic Cash System."

This was the first Bitcoin transaction, but few people noticed it at the time. Through most of 2009, no one would value a single Bitcoin at more than just a few pennies. In 2010 a programmer completed the first known commercial Bitcoin transaction: the delivery of two pizzas for 10,000 Bitcoins. Seven years later, the Bitcoin used to buy those two pizzas was worth more than $100 million. The day that the transaction

Although Bitcoin is a form of digital currency, some physical coins have been produced as collectors' items. The physical coin can come preloaded with the code for a digital Bitcoin or can come blank so that buyers can upload their own Bitcoin to it.

occurred—May 22—would be celebrated by cryptocurrency enthusiasts as a holiday: Bitcoin Pizza Day.

The journey of Bitcoin, from an obscure program to the height of global finance, is an extraordinary and controversial story. Bitcoin is the most well-known cryptocurrency. A cryptocurrency, in simple terms, is a digital asset that relies on the internet and computers to verify its value and ownership. It is designed to be used like money. According to supporters, cryptocurrencies represent a new way of storing value and conducting business, one that exploits the ease and reach of technology. In this vision, cryptocurrencies will replace paper and coin currencies. Costly, slow intermediaries will be removed from the transaction process. Tyrannical governments and corrupt institutions will be sidelined. Individuals will freely conduct transactions directly with one another in a framework that establishes and maintains trust.

At the heart of these claims lies the infrastructure beneath Bitcoin: blockchain. Blockchain is a decentralized computer system that can guarantee the authenticity of data. In effect, blockchain establishes the truth. Blockchain can validate transactions between organizations or people—from concert tickets, to supply chains, to legal documents such as property deeds, stock certificates, or identification cards.

These extraordinary claims have drawn skepticism from economists, technology experts, and financial regulators. They deride cryptocurrencies as at best a fad and at worst a fraud. In their view, Bitcoin and its herd of copycats are driven by speculators hoping to bid up prices before dumping them, leaving investors with losses. Blockchain ignores the value and stability that intermediaries bring to society and requires a deep understanding of computer code. It assumes technology can solve human nature.

Who is right? We'll find out, because if there's anything certain about Bitcoin, cryptocurrencies, and blockchain, it's that they are not going away anytime soon. Rather, they are at the center of debates about the role of technology in human society. Cryptocurrencies and blockchain can play a critical role in the future—for better or for worse.

CHAPTER 1

BITCOIN AND BLOCKCHAIN

Money is an essential component of civilization. It acts as a medium of exchange for individuals, enabling them to buy and sell goods and services. When it functions properly, money also allows individuals to store value over time.

Over thousands of years, people have employed many different kinds of money—from beads to metal coins and from shells to coffee beans. Some forms of money are more effective than others. "To be a really good currency," wrote economist and *Financial Times* columnist Martin Wolf, "it needs to be durable, portable, divisible, uniform, limited in supply, and acceptable."

Today, most people use fiat money, or what we would recognize as coins and paper bills. Fiat money is made legal tender, or currency, by government regulation. This money actually has no intrinsic value on its own. People give and receive money for real goods and services because it is a socially accepted symbol of value. Citizens must also use it to pay their taxes.

However, it can be unnerving to realize that fiat money is based mostly on trust. Citizens have to believe that the government won't simply make more when it needs to.

There is no way to track the origins and history of a paper bill, making it much easier to counterfeit than cryptocurrency coins, each of which can be fully tracked on the blockchain.

When the government prints too much money, inflation rises. The value of the currency declines because it doesn't buy as much as it used to. Hyperinflation occurs when the currency loses its value. When a society loses faith in its currency, the results can be catastrophic. Citizens can't afford food, savings are destroyed, and law and order breaks down.

"The root problem with conventional currency is all the trust that's required to make it work," said researchers Stanton Heister and Kristi

Yuthas. "The central bank must be trusted not to debase the currency, but the history of fiat currencies is full of breaches of trust."

Some critics believe that governments, inevitably, will print money to solve short-term problems or meet immediate needs. These people are often skeptical of government in general, which they argue has too much power—to print money, collect it, and monitor it. Some people believe that the government won't properly oversee the financial system, which is charged with holding savings, making loans, and investing. If the government fails in this role, citizens' savings would be jeopardized.

All of these fears appeared to come true during the global financial crisis of 2007–2008. In January 2009, the global financial system was near collapse. In the United States, millions of home mortgages had been given to people who were unable to repay them. These mortgages had been repackaged into securities that had been sold to banks and other financial institutions around the world. When the home mortgages soured, financial firms began to implode.

Governments were forced to spend hundreds of billions of dollars to prop up financial institutions to avoid a catastrophic economic depression. The bailouts were controversial. Families lost their homes, and investors lost fortunes. But the CEOs who ran these companies seemed to largely escape punishment. The global financial crisis of 2007–2008 eroded trust across society—in government, institutions, and individuals.

In the very first Bitcoin transaction, Satoshi Nakamoto quoted the title of a story in the *London Times* from January 3, 2009: "Chancellor on Brink of Second Bailout for Banks." With this reference, Nakamoto summed up the issues that led them to launch Bitcoin. They didn't have to make a case. They only had to point to the global financial crisis of 2007–2008, which led many people to an extreme conclusion: governments can't be trusted with money.

Bitcoin was Nakamoto's answer to the challenges of fiat money. It could be easily stored, instantly transmitted, and verifiable through a simple process.

WHO IS SATOSHI NAKAMOTO?

Satoshi Nakamoto could be an individual or a group of people (this book refers to Nakamoto as "they"). They have not publicly released their true identity. Some believed Nakamoto mined approximately 1 million Bitcoin and, in 2010 handed over control of the network. Except for a few cryptic messages, they haven't been heard from since. A number of individuals have claimed they are Nakamoto, but no one has been able to prove it.

No one knows who Nakamoto truly is—or if they are even a real person.

As technology journalist Brian Patrick Eha said, "Bitcoin looks like money's dream of itself."

DIGITAL CURRENCY: A PROBLEM AND A SOLUTION

To create Bitcoin, Nakamoto had to overcome an enormous challenge: anything on the internet can be easily copied. Money has value, in part, because its supply is limited. If all the gold in the world was gathered together, it would make a cube less than 75 feet (23 m) on each side. If someone were able to cheaply create gold in a laboratory, though, it would quickly lose value.

There are many ways in which creators of a product deliberately limit supply. In the late 1990s, music was primarily available only on compact discs (CDs). If you wanted a song, you had to buy an individual copy, which you usually got only if you purchased the whole album. Once you owned the CD, you could not make copies. If you wanted to share the song with a friend, they had to borrow your CD (in which case you couldn't listen to it). This was also true of most other forms of media—newspapers, books, and DVDs. It is no surprise that these industries enjoyed strong profits in the late 1990s.

The internet, however, destroyed this model. New websites allowed users to download entire movies and to share music files. One person could simply buy a song and make an enormous number of copies to share with friends at no additional cost. Once newspapers posted stories online in digital form, they could be easily copied and reproduced elsewhere.

ENSURING SCARCITY

The value of something is often determined by the amount of it (supply) versus the desire people have for it (demand). If something is rare and highly desirable (such as a house on a beach), then it will carry a high price. If something is common (such as sand) and exceeds demand, then the price will be low. Fiat currencies usually lose trust when governments print too much of it, causing it to lose value.

Satoshi Nakamoto designed Bitcoin so only a finite number exist. The number of coins in circulation will top out at 21 million in 2140. Of the 21 million Bitcoin units that will be released, 18 million are already in circulation.

Music sales dropped by more than half over the next fifteen years. Many newspapers were forced to merge or close. Writers and musicians struggled to generate new revenue from their work. Anything that could be digitized could be infinitely reproduced at no cost, effectively making it worthless. The internet, it turns out, was extremely good at transferring information and, in doing so, destroying value.

Given this reality, how could a digital currency exist? A ten-dollar bill in your pocket can't be reproduced. If you lose it, it's gone. If you use it to buy goods, the person receiving the money can trust that it's real money. A digital currency is just a computer file. It could simply be reproduced by the holder and used repeatedly. Bitcoin, however, achieved something extraordinary in the digital world: it's almost impossible to counterfeit the coins. Nakamoto accomplished this through blockchain.

THE BASICS OF BLOCKCHAIN

Blockchain is an online ledger, or a list of records. It identifies who owns something at any given time. One group of Chinese blockchain experts called it "the latest and most trustworthy form of bookkeeping." Each record is time-stamped and combined with other records via cryptography to create a block. The blocks are independently checked and validated by a peer-to-peer network, which consists of independent computers all over the world. They combine the blocks into a chain (hence the "blockchain"), including the most recent transactions.

If you wanted to pass a file to a friend, the blockchain would establish that you are the current owner and then confirm the new owner. The peer-to-peer network would validate the transaction and update the blockchain. The file can't be copied and distributed to anyone else. There is only one file. Thus, blockchain effectively solves the problem of digitization and makes a digital currency possible.

"A blockchain is like the digital version of a scarf knitted by your grandmother," wrote New Yorker reporter Nathan Heller. "She uses one

HOW A BLOCKCHAIN TRANSACTION WORKS

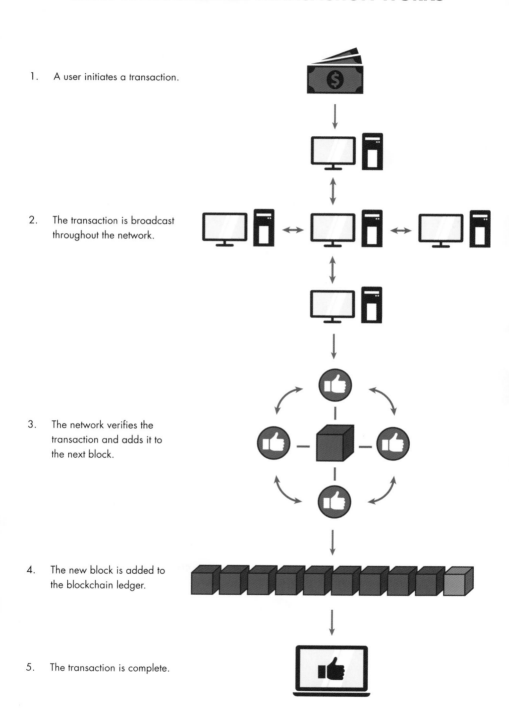

1. A user initiates a transaction.

2. The transaction is broadcast throughout the network.

3. The network verifies the transaction and adds it to the next block.

4. The new block is added to the blockchain ledger.

5. The transaction is complete.

ball of yarn, and the result is continuous. Each stitch depends on the one just before it. It's impossible to remove part of the fabric, or to substitute a swatch, without leaving some trace: a few telling knots, or a change in the knit. In a blockchain system, too, every line is contingent on what came before it. Any breach of the weave leaves a trace, and trying to cover your tracks leaves a trace too."

THE BITCOIN BLOCKCHAIN

Bitcoin is the most well-known and successful application of blockchain. Studying Bitcoin leads to a better understanding of how blockchain works in the real world.

Bitcoin accounts are called addresses. They are random strings of letters and numbers. Nothing else is associated with them—no names, no social security numbers, and no business or residential addresses that would identify the owner. Each Bitcoin address has a secret code, or a private key, that allows someone to access it. The owner of the secret code holds the Bitcoin. If the secret code is stolen, forgotten, or otherwise lost, the Bitcoin cannot be used.

The holder transfers the Bitcoin to another person by using their private key. The transaction actually becomes part of the Bitcoin code and is transparent, meaning anyone with access to a computer or smartphone can see which addresses have owned the Bitcoin and which address owns it currently.

Nakamoto created incentives for third parties to verify Bitcoin transactions. The verification involves solving a complicated math problem—or proof of work—that requires significant computing power and energy. The third parties, called miners, are compensated for their work by being paid a fraction of the transaction in Bitcoin. They also receive a block reward, or a certain quantity of newly generated Bitcoin. The miners race to validate the transactions, and the reward goes to the miner who completes the proof of work the fastest and most thoroughly.

Many miners use cooling devices and fans to keep their computers from overheating. In addition to using a lot of power and racking up the energy bill, mining requires powerful processors that ordinary personal computers don't come with.

Each transaction is recorded through an algorithm that takes its details—time, amounts, and sender and recipient addresses—and converts the transaction into a string of letters and numbers called a hash. Anyone running the information through the algorithm will come back with the same hash. Each hash can be combined with another, resulting in a new hash that embodies both. Thus, when a miner adds a block to the blockchain, it is linked to a chain of hashes that go back all the way to the first, or "Genesis," block launched by Nakamoto on January 3, 2009.

Any alteration to the chain, no matter how insignificant, results in a completely different hash. Consequently, the record of a transaction cannot be changed because many independent parties have already confirmed the information. After a miner verifies the transaction, other computers on the peer-to-peer network, called nodes, will validate the miner's work with the original blockchain. If a node detects an irregularity, they will not attach a new block to it. Rather, they will go back to an earlier part of the chain that can be trusted and attach it there. The rejected block becomes an "orphan." Orphans also result from situations where two miners solve the proof-of-work problem at the same time—the network has to choose one of the two blocks, and the rejected one becomes an orphan. Because of this process, any blockchain user

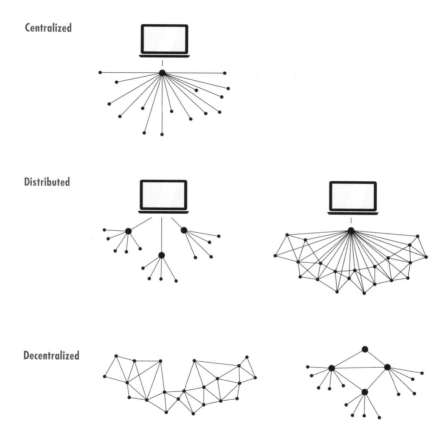

Centralized

Distributed

Decentralized

This diagram illustrates three types of organization: centralized, distributed, and decentralized. A decentralized structure distributes decision-making power and authority across a large group of people. In a centralized system, most of the authority belongs to a single, central entity, such as a government or a corporation. Finally, distributed systems consist of nodes that coordinate their computing to reach a consensus; they can be either centralized or decentralized.

can trust the ledger's information because the peer-to-peer network has already confirmed it.

Nakamoto designed Bitcoin so it would take about ten minutes to mine each block. Sometimes, though, it can take just a few minutes or as long as an hour. If many Bitcoins are being mined and require more computing power, Nakamoto's algorithms automatically adjust, making them easier to mine. However, if fewer blocks are being mined, the difficulty is increased. The goal is to maintain a mining time of ten minutes per block.

The value of a Bitcoin depends on the trust it generates among everyone who uses it—in investors, in users, and in society at large. As a result, Bitcoin miners have an incentive to be honest and to validate the transactions. If anyone commits fraud with the system and destroys trust, all Bitcoins become worthless.

"And so, a central authority is replaced by a network of volunteers pursuing their own self-interest," wrote blockchain expert Omid Malekan.

Through Bitcoin, Nakamoto demonstrated the viability of blockchain. Over the years that followed, computer scientists, investors, regulators, governments, experts, economists, and ordinary citizens grappled with this new system and its implications.

"There is great confusion and debate about what a blockchain even is," wrote tech journalist Gideon Lewis-Kraus, "but the standard definition describes a shared, decentralized, cryptographically secure, immutable digital ledger. In the broadest terms, a blockchain allows a group of strangers to agree on a state of affairs, and to proceed together on the basis of the covenant."

This language makes blockchain sound bland, but blockchain's supporters believe it reveals how revolutionary blockchain could be. To them, "a group of strangers" who "agree on a state of affairs, and proceed together on the basis of the covenant" sounds like the beginning of a civilization.

Marc Andreessen, a venture capitalist who launched the first popular internet browser in the early 1990s and was a cofounder of Netscape, wrote in the *New York Times* that Bitcoin was the next big thing:

> A mysterious new technology emerges, seemingly out of nowhere, but actually the result of two decades of intense research and development by nearly anonymous researchers.
>
> Political idealists project visions of liberation and revolution onto it; establishment elites heap contempt and scorn on it.
>
> On the other hand, technologists—nerds—are transfixed by it. They see within it enormous potential and spend nights and weekends tinkering with it.
>
> What technology am I talking about? Personal computers in 1975, the internet in 1993, and—I believe—Bitcoin in 2014.

CHAPTER 2

ESTABLISHING POTENTIAL

Trade is based on trust, which can be difficult to build and easy to break. Who am I trading with? How do I know that I'm going to get what I traded for? Will the other party honor our agreement? In contemporary society, these problems are often

In modern financial systems, massive institutions such as banks, law firms, and brokerage houses guarantee transactions. A consumer orders a shirt online, and the bank confirms to the vendor that the consumer can pay for it. Intermediaries ensure the package is delivered and the payment is received.

It can be easy to forget how complicated these transactions can be. A person can't buy something until they are certain that the seller actually owns it. At each stage, ownership has to be established—that the seller possesses the goods to be sold and the buyer possesses the means to pay for it. The agreement must be made by both sides and confirmed by the intermediary.

For larger and more complicated transactions, it should be noted, the intermediary could fail. Clerks can make mistakes, documents can be lost, titles can be forged, and officials can be bribed to change records. In the global financial crisis of 2007–2008, banks failed to verify that new owners could pay for the houses they bought.

Blockchain, however, removes this uncertainty. Ownership of an asset is independently confirmed through the blockchain ledger. Since the ledger exists in copies distributed all over the world, it is extremely difficult—if not impossible—to alter it without detection. In addition, if one part of the network fails, the ledger that proves ownership will still exist in other parts of the network. This decentralized network is thus safe from a single person, or regime, seeking to shut it down.

ELIMINATING THE INTERMEDIARY

By establishing proof of ownership, the blockchain removes the intermediary, which can bring many benefits. "We pay these centralized entities handsomely for their custodial services, not only in the form of rents they charge but in the control they exert over our lives," wrote tech journalist Gideon Lewis-Kraus. "The blockchain, in theory, affords us new opportunities to solve complex coordination problems without letting the incumbent coordinators extract so much value in the process."

Consider something as simple as buying tickets to a sports event. Many people use a popular website to buy tickets. The website establishes that the ticket actually exists, confirms the exchange of the ticket between two parties, and then has a mechanism for delivery. For these services, the website, acting as an intermediary, adds a hefty fee, increasing the cost of the ticket significantly.

On blockchain, however, the ticket would be assigned a public address. The owner holds the private key that gives her access to the address. When the owner sells the ticket, a new address is created for the ticket and added to the blockchain. The new owner receives a new private key that establishes her ownership of the ticket. No intermediary is

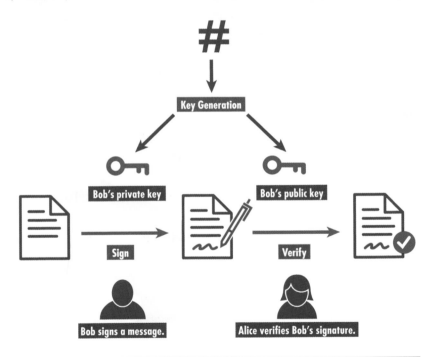

This illustration shows how two people use each other's keys to verify ownership and conduct a transaction. To begin, Bob uses a key generation function to transform a big, random number into two keys: a private key and a public key. He uses his private key to encrypt some information and then sends the information to Alice. Alice, on the other end of the transaction, uses Bob's public key to decrypt the message. Because the two keys were made by the same mathematical function, they are related to each other, so the public key verifies Bob's private key without revealing it to Alice.

needed, and no fee is added to the ticket's cost. As an added bonus, the transaction is virtually instantaneous.

Banks are the ultimate intermediary. Blockchain supporters believe blockchain-based applications could replace vast portions of the current financial system. New companies that need funding could issue tokens rather than stock. Houses could be bought and sold without the extensive due diligence required today.

Banking has grown much more convenient over the past two decades with the creation of cash machines and online banking. But the underlying system has changed remarkably little. It still takes twenty-four hours to wire money. The routing number at the bottom of paper checks was first developed a century ago. Even credit card transactions can take several minutes to settle. Many blockchain transactions, in comparison, take seconds.

Another area of the global economy crowded with intermediaries is trade. This system can introduce inconsistencies, lead to errors, and offer opportunities for fraud. In October 2015, a number of Chipotle customers fell ill from *E. coli* bacteria. As customers fled and the company's stock price plunged, management frantically searched for the source of the outbreak. The investigation, however, stalled. After five months, the company reported that contaminated meat from Australia was the likely source. They could not be more precise than that.

The problem is that companies work with many suppliers, and these suppliers are often incentivized not to work together. In fact, they often compete for business from the larger company. As a result, information can be inaccessible to other members of the supply chain, or even to the company making the orders. Managers at a number of restaurant chains have no way of confirming the food they receive meets agreed-upon standards.

As conservation biologist Guillaume Chapron stated, "One reason why we have environmental crises, like the overexploitation of natural resources, and pollution, is because the global economy is full of actors who are doing business without much accountability. When you go buy something, you have no idea where it comes from, how it's made. There are so many intermediaries, and it's very easy to cheat."

Blockchain, however, provides a time-stamped log of each transaction. The log is transparent and cannot be changed without alerting all the other people on the network. For example, when transporting food, the information in the log may include storage temperature and location, why the item was moved, and even whether the truck transporting the products shook too much (which can cause a significant loss of shelf life for some products—think bruised apples). As a result, blockchain can allow strangers with different goals to establish trust and work together. The ultimate goal is transparency that does not compromise each company's competitive information. Moreover, blockchain establishes a standard ledger between parties that covers the details of a transaction from origin to delivery. While this structure by itself won't eliminate fraud (after all, someone could deliberately enter false records), it establishes consistency in record keeping. Some of the largest companies in the world, such as IBM, Walmart, Carrefour, and Tyson Foods, have explored how they can use blockchain technology.

Even some relatively small companies are already using blockchain. For example, on a ranch in northern Wyoming, a few hundred calves are logged to a blockchain. The blockchain allows the rancher—who raises his animals on open grassland—to prove to customers that his meat is higher quality and is raised humanely. Typically, tracking is a paper-intensive process with multiple places for errors or fraud as cows are traded and moved from one spot to another. Blockchain addresses these challenges in tracking beef.

Blockchain technology may give diners an intimate portrait of the chicken they are about to eat. A chicken can wear a device on its foot that tracks it through the supply chain from farm to plate. Information about each chicken is uploaded to a blockchain. Diners downloading this information via an app to their smartphones could become the new norm. Blockchain could even come to supermarkets—one shopper recalls being able to scan a box of berries and see the family that grew them.

At a conference in New York City in 2018, tuna sushi was served to attendees. Each napkin had a QR code that the attendee could scan with a smartphone. The code then showed them, via blockchain, how the fish was caught off the island of Fiji in the South Pacific, as well as how it was tagged with an ID and tracked as each individual piece was transported over thousands of miles to their plates.

Blockchain can be used for more than just commerce. Environmental causes often fail because supporters are not certain how their donation is being used, or whether a product is genuinely favorable to the environment. One group, Plastic Bank, tries to reduce the amount of plastic that enters the world's oceans, where it has become a serious source of pollution. Plastic Bank pays individuals tokens for redeemed plastic bottles and other plastic waste. It then resells the plastic at a premium to manufacturing companies, which attracts environmentally aware consumers. Blockchain is essential to each part of this process. It guarantees payment for pieces of plastic, often in societies with no banking or high crime rates. It ensures that the plastic used in the recycled products is *actually* recycled, assuring the end user their purchase has helped support an environmental cause.

SMART CONTRACTS

As Bitcoin became more popular, a young Russian Canadian named Vitalik Buterin became excited by the potential to apply blockchain technology to a much larger range of transactions. Buterin was the son of a computer scientist from Grozny in Chechnya, a republic in southwestern Russia that was mostly destroyed in the 1990s when Russian troops fought bitter urban battles with separatists. His father immigrated to

Canada when Buterin was six, and he inherited much of his father's disgust for governments and the havoc they could wreak.

"I saw everything to do with either government regulation or corporate control as just being plain evil," Buterin told a *New Yorker* reporter, "and I assumed that people in those institutions were kind of like Mr. Burns [Homer Simpson's greedy boss in *The Simpsons*], sitting behind their desks saying, 'Excellent. How can I screw a thousand people over this time?'"

Buterin was also attracted to the individuals who were creating a new decentralized system. "Their earlier pedigrees, if they had any pedigrees at all, were in open source—Linux, Mozilla, and cypherpunk mailing lists," he said. "I found it immensely empowering that just a few thousand people like myself could re-create this fundamental social institution from nothing."

Buterin admired Bitcoin, but he wanted to

Buterin speaks at TechCrunch Disrupt, a technology conference, in 2015. Buterin received a fellowship award of $100,000 in 2014 that he used to help fund Ethereum.

do more than simply process transactions based on a digital currency. He wanted to create a peer-to-peer network that accomplished tasks. These tasks were set out in agreements called smart contracts.

Smart contracts can connect to several blockchains and execute agreements without the need for human interaction. Smart contracts could be used for a guaranteed transaction that is based on timing, such as renting an apartment. The renter pays in Bitcoin, which releases a code providing access to the apartment. If the landlord doesn't send the code by a certain time, then the Bitcoin is refunded to the renter. The smart contract automatically verifies all pieces of the transaction through the decentralized peer-to-peer network. This includes the landlord's ownership of the apartment and the tenant's possession of the Bitcoin to pay for it. This process eliminates the intermediaries, such as banks, and saves both the renter and the landlord money and time.

In 2015, Buterin launched the Ethereum platform, which uses a cryptocurrency called Ether to pay the computers on the peer-to-peer network to execute smart contracts. Buterin described his creation as "Android for decentralized apps"—leading him to call the smart contracts "Dapps." Buterin compared Ethereum to a smartphone that is programmed to perform the apps (or "Dapps") on its platform. In effect, programmers on Ethereum had access to a decentralized supercomputer.

"If it lived up to all that Buterin and others imagined," wrote digital currency experts Michael Casey and Paul Vigna, "the system would amount to a global decentralized virtual machine, one that always implemented users' coding instructions without any control by any one computer."

Buterin and many blockchain supporters hoped Ethereum and other blockchain platforms would help address a major problem. Most people's experiences on the internet were absorbed onto massive platforms such as Google, Facebook, and Amazon. The platforms had started out as places where people could simply carry out tasks, such as "search" or "buy an item," or connect with another person or group. But over time, the platforms appeared more and more to be dictating these experiences. Through tracking and gathering of data, they used algorithms to deliver information and advertisements to users. Worse, they demanded the user surrender their personal information to have access to the platform. Many hoped that blockchain could eliminate these intermediaries and restore the original promise of the internet.

CHAPTER 3

CRYPTO-CURRENCIES TAKE OFF

At first, many people were attracted to Bitcoin for one reason: anonymity. In February 2011, the Silk Road Dark Web opened. It offered various illegal goods and services, including drugs, stolen identities and passwords, weapons, and sex trafficking. It accepted payment in Bitcoin only. At that time, one Bitcoin was worth about thirty cents. Critics dismissed Bitcoin as the currency of choice for criminals and terrorists, but some investors noticed that Bitcoin's premise was holding true. It allowed strangers—even criminals—to establish trust and conduct transactions. In short, Bitcoin was working the way its creators intended.

This attracted attention, especially as Bitcoin's price began a series of dramatic rises and falls. For speculators, Bitcoin appeared to be an opportunity to make a lot of money fast. Law enforcement also began investigations. In the spring of 2013, the US government took down the Silk Road Dark Web bazaar and confiscated more than 150,000 Bitcoins.

Bitcoin, and cryptocurrencies in general, preoccupied government regulators. Regulators are charged with enforcing government rules, especially in finance. At the time, other tech-based services such as Airbnb and Uber were causing a huge disruption in the taxi and hotel industries. Taxi services and hotel companies were forced to compete with drivers and apartment owners who, through the internet, could connect directly with customers.

Regulators wondered if this could also happen to finance. At conferences, they asked nervous questions. Are cryptocurrencies a fraud? What impact could they have on financial institutions? Could cryptocurrencies break the government monopoly on money? US authorities seized cryptocurrency accounts that had traded without being properly registered with federal agencies. China also cracked down, declaring that no financial institution could use cryptocurrencies (although citizens still could). The price of Bitcoin rose and fell with these announcements, but the general trend was higher. At the start of 2014, the value of Bitcoin shot up from about $13 to $770 per coin.

Bitcoin stories now appeared regularly on news shows and in headlines. Bitcoin holders, who had once swapped them for pennies and begged anyone to notice them, were making fortunes. Bitcoin had arrived.

All around the world, cryptocurrencies attracted those who saw a chance to make a fast fortune. South Korea became the third-largest market in cryptocurrency, after the United States and Japan. Poor, young Koreans called themselves dirty spoons. The name was based on the contrast between them and the elite who were said to have silver and gold spoons because of their jobs, wealth, and opportunity. To the dirty spoons, cryptocurrencies seemed a chance to make good money and potentially upend a social order that seemed stifling. They could buy cryptocurrencies even when they had no chance to buy stocks or get a loan to fund a business.

One dirty spoon, twenty-nine-year-old Remy Kim, hosted social media channels on cryptocurrencies. He first learned about them when a hacker took over his hard drive and demanded ransom in Bitcoin. Kim came up with the 1.2 Bitcoins (then worth about $800), but he grew fascinated by the cryptocurrency and bought some Bitcoin for himself. As the market rose, he bought a navy-blue Rolls Royce worth $500,000. Online, he took the name Les Mis, after the musical and novel *Les Misérables*, in which the poor rise up to overthrow a corrupt and brutal government.

Bitcoin's rise became parabolic. It started 2017 worth just below $1,000. Over the summer, its value broke $4,000. By mid-December, the value had soared above $19,000.

In New York City, an open-air Bitcoin market opened up in Union Square. People gathered under a statue of Abraham Lincoln, and they had backpacks full of cash and bid for the digital coins. The market, renamed Satoshi Square, and its participants were reminiscent of the first New York traders centuries ago, who gathered in open areas near Wall Street.

Bitcoin machines, called BTMs, began to appear. About four thousand were in use around the world by the end of 2018, with more than two thousand in the United States alone. In New York City, 110 stores offered a Bitcoin machine. One estimate claimed that five new Bitcoin machines were installed each day. Money could easily be deposited and then converted into Bitcoin in a digital wallet that was instantly accessible from anywhere in the world.

Those who were lucky—or smart—enough to take a chance on Bitcoin in its infancy grew rich. One twelve-year-old, Erik Finman,

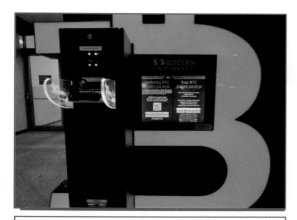
This BTM sits in a train station in Poland.

borrowed $1,000 from his grandmother to buy Bitcoin when it was $10 per coin. He was later offered $100,000, or 300 Bitcoin, for video technology he had developed. He accepted Bitcoin, and his wealth compounded. Finman, who hated school, convinced his parents to agree to a deal: if he made $1 million before he turned eighteen, he wouldn't have to attend college. He won the deal.

Cryptocurrency holders, now worth more money than they had once dared to dream, became very protective of their identities. It wouldn't take much for a person with a gun to simply demand their passwords. Journalist Nellie Bowles noted that, considering blockchain is supposed to provide security on the internet, people who hold cryptocurrencies appeared to be very insecure. "There's a common paranoia among the crypto wealthy that they'll be targeted and robbed since there's no bank securing the money, so many are obsessively secretive," she wrote. Conspicuous consumption of wealth was discouraged among cryptocurrency holders, though a few exceptions applied. Purchases of Lamborghinis—or Lambos—were celebrated.

As Bitcoin prices rose, some jubilant holders planned to cash in, only to find that they had lost their private keys. One IT worker mined over 7,500 coins in 2009. "There were just six of us doing it at the time," he noted, "and it was like the early days of a gold rush." He stored his private keys to the coins on a hard drive that sat in his desk drawer.

"Four years later, I had two hard drives in a desk drawer. One was empty and the other contained my Bitcoin private keys," he recalled. "I meant to throw away the empty drive—and I accidentally threw away the one with the Bitcoin information." By that time, his Bitcoin were worth $60 million. He begged his town to let him excavate the landfill where his hard drive was likely dumped. They refused.

Another Bitcoin holder, Mark Frauenfelder, spent $3,000 on 7.4 Bitcoins that he stored on a hardware wallet, a secure hardware device. As part of the security procedure, the wallet, called Trezor, generated twenty-four random words that he wrote down on a piece of paper and stored in his desk drawer. If he lost the Trezor, he could simply get a new one and use the twenty-four words to access his account. Just before a trip to Tokyo, Frauenfelder decided to put the paper beneath his daughter's pillow in case he died in an accident. Bitcoin was rising fast, and he wanted his daughter to have access to the money. His daughter, however, was in London at the time and didn't return for another week. In the meantime, his cleaning service went through the apartment, found the piece of paper with obscure names all over it and threw it away.

When Frauenfelder discovered the error, he thought it would be a minor inconvenience. He still knew his PIN, which would allow him to generate a new account and transfer the Bitcoins over. But when

BITCOIN OBLIVION

No one likes passwords, and Bitcoin passwords are virtually impossible to memorize. One cryptocurrency developer estimates that of the 21 million Bitcoins in existence, as many as 4 million may be lost.

These are some examples of cryptokitties. Each kitty is a unique combination of features, making it hypothetically valuable.

Frauenfelder tried the PIN, Trezor kept rejecting it. Frauenfelder tried dozens of variations. Nothing worked.

"I felt queasy," he recalled. "After my sixth incorrect PIN attempt, creeping dread had escalated to heart-pounding panic—I might have kissed my 7.4 Bitcoins goodbye."

Frauenfelder continued to try PINs; he kept failing. "This decentralized nature of the Bitcoin network is not without consequences—the main one being that if you screw up, it's your own damn problem," he noted ruefully.

These stories, however, did little to suppress what had become an investing craze. The Long Island Iced Tea Company changed its name to Long Blockchain Company. Its stock rose 500 percent in a single day.

A blockchain game allowed users to produce, or breed, a cryptokitty—a computer graphic image of a cat. Because each image was unique, scarcity occurred, which drove up prices. Users could only pay via Ether, and one kitty, Dragon, reportedly sold for $170,000.

Jonas Lund, a thirty-four-year-old Swedish artist, used blockchain to create 100,000 Jonas Lund Tokens (JLTs). He gave these tokens to a board of trustees, who used them to vote on what artistic and professional steps

Hillside Public Library

Lund should take. In one instance, Lund had four ideas for artistically transforming a piece of plywood: with an engraving, with metallic gray paint, with pictures of birds and bullet points explaining his process, or with paint and then fire "in a controlled way to create something very fragile." Lund asked his board of trustees what he should do. They used their tokens to select the third option: pictures of birds. This selection will correlate to 1,041 tokens in the future. When someone buys the piece, they will be awarded the tokens, which they can then use to vote on the direction of Lund's art.

With the blockchain-based tokens, Lund is simply formalizing what he sees as the personal, market, and community forces that influence art. Lund has given the tokens to people he knows, and some people were awarded tokens for buying his work. He also offers tokens to individuals who invite him to a talk, tweet about him, or use the hashtag #jonaslundtoken.

ARE DIGITAL COINS SECURITIES?

An important issue for cryptocurrencies and blockchain is whether a digital coin, or token, is actually a security, or a tradable financial asset. If a digital coin is a security, then it comes under a legal classification that is regulated by the US government. The US Securities and Exchange Commission (SEC) was set up after the Wall Street crash of 1929, a historic event that wiped out stockholders and ushered in the Great Depression (1929–1942). In practical terms, the SEC is charged with ensuring that investors have some transparency into securities markets and can better avoid abuse and fraud. If cyrptocurrencies are considered securities, then they would be heavily regulated, potentially removing many of the features—such as anonymity—that made them so attractive in the first place.

Everyone, it seemed, was talking about cryptocurrencies. But regulators remained skeptical. Crypto supporters, or cryptobros, urged the SEC to approve a Bitcoin exchange traded fund (ETF). "Adapt or die," wrote one supporter. "Approve Bitcoin ETF and take the leading step for advancing the human race through the revolutionary technology we have been gifted."

In July 2017, Ethereum was two years old. The price of Ether had risen from $8 to $400 in the first half of 2017, giving many people plenty of reasons to celebrate. An anniversary party for the coin drew three hundred people to a rooftop bar in Manhattan. Michael Casey and Paul Vigna attended, noting that they had witnessed many of the booms and busts in the city, from the dot.com craze in the late 1990s to Bitcoin. The scene, they said, was virtually the same.

"The energy of the crowd was palpable," the journalists wrote. "The expectations of instant wealth unmistakable. Like most other tech breakthroughs, this one contained a mixture of utopianism and capitalism. Some people wanted to change the world. Some wanted to get rich. Many imagined they could do both."

In 2017 initial coin offerings (ICOs) drew exuberant attention. Digital companies issued their own coin, and investors hoping to enjoy the returns realized by the first Bitcoin owners piled in. These companies raised $6.6 billion in 2017. Dozens of coins or tokens appeared, many of them variations on Bitcoin called altcoins. EOS, "the most powerful application for decentralized applications," raised $4.2 billion. TaTaTu, "social entertainment on the blockchain," attracted $575 million. Dragon, "the entertainment token," raised $420 million.

In 2018, a Ukrainian social media network wanted to raise publicity for its ICO. It decided to send four crypto enthusiasts to the top of Mt. Everest where they would bury a hard drive containing cryptocurrencies at the summit. Two of the climbers never reached the summit. The other two reached the peak and were trapped in bad weather. They were later evacuated and treated for frostbite. One Sherpa accompanying them died. The company, ASKfm, reported that the hard drive supposedly had 50,000 worth of cryptocoins on it, and they encouraged others to search for it.

Stunts like this attracted negative publicity, and many critics continued to see cryptocurrencies as little more than a tool for criminals. People hesitated to use them as a medium of exchange because, according to economist Martin Wolf, "law-abiding people and businesses do not want to own assets that are, by virtue of their anonymity, ideal for criminals, terrorists and money launderers."

Other critics focused on cryptocurrencies' volatility, as well as the controversies that hit the more established digital coins, especially related to security. "None of that is encouraging for anyone who needs a currency to reliably pay for groceries and rent," noted columnist Lionel Laurent.

BITCOIN AND GOOGLE SEARCHES

Google reported that "how to buy Bitcoin" was the third-highest "how-to" search in 2017 (the top search was "how to make slime"). In some countries, Google searches for "Bitcoin" exceeded searches for "gold." This was true for countries where confidence in the central government was low, such as Algeria, Colombia, and Venezuela. In 2019 interest in Bitcoin was especially high in Nigeria and South Africa, both of which had experienced currency devaluations. Citizens of these countries were also very uncertain about their governments, especially the prospects for economic reforms.

A FORK IN THE BLOCKCHAIN

As Bitcoin transactions became more frequent, they also became more expensive. Bitcoin transactions were hardwired to be limited to one megabyte. Because of this small size, the blockchain network only processed seven transactions per second. By comparison, credit card companies can handle more than fifty thousand transactions per second. As more and more Bitcoin transactions were processed, the network became clogged.

Some users offered miners higher fees to include their transaction in a block. By 2017 users were paying miners an average of five dollars per transaction. This made small transactions prohibitively expensive—buyers of movie tickets or a cup of coffee would have to pay five dollars extra. Worse, to blockchain supporters, the preferential system was starting to resemble the system of intermediaries—banks, agencies, and so on—that blockchain was trying to replace. Users who wanted to pay cheaper fees found they had to wait hours, or even days, to have their transactions processed.

An obvious solution was to make the transaction sizes larger, but miners protested that these would cost more to process. If costs rose, fewer miners would participate, potentially making the system more vulnerable to manipulation. One side wanted greater ease and convenience. The other stressed security.

The debate grew acrimonious. One group proposed a "fork" to Bitcoin. A fork occurs when two miners solve the proof of work in a blockchain almost simultaneously, resulting in a discrepancy in the ledger. In effect, the two transactions present a fork in the ledger, offering two potential outcomes for the ledger to follow. At this point, a consensus mechanism in the community selects the most accurate transaction, leaving the other transaction to be ignored. The fork is then resolved.

Forks, however, can allow the community of miners and nodes to effectively change the rules of the blockchain. The challenge is to get the blockchain community to agree to the change. After all, there is no centralized decision-making body that can simply order everyone to obey its decrees. Rather, the community has to come to a consensus.

Forks can be either soft or hard. In simple terms, a soft fork limits a blockchain's rules going forward, while a hard fork expands them. A soft fork is much like an upgrade to a piece of software. Just as an upgraded computer can still run older versions of software, the blockchain can still work with miners and nodes who haven't upgraded. A soft fork only requires a majority of a blockchain's users to approve. A hard fork, however, is more difficult because it splits the blockchain into two incompatible chains, one that follows the old rules and one that follows a new set of rules. As a result, a hard fork requires unanimous agreement from a blockchain's users. Otherwise, two different timelines for a blockchain will come into existence. In effect, one group will observe one set of rules, while the other will obey the other set.

One software developer proposed a soft fork to the Bitcoin blockchain that would make it more efficient to process more content, effectively

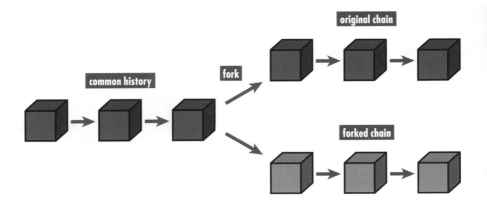

This diagram shows how each branch of a blockchain fork shares a common history, but one branch will follow a new set of rules, while the other follows the original rules. In a hard fork, the rules are so different that the two chains are incompatible.

doubling its capacity. The fork would also allow Bitcoin to be used on a new network called Lightning. The Lightning Network allowed users to sign contracts that enabled them to use two-payment channels according to a preestablished balance. More important, the system allowed users to transfer funds to third parties without the need for miners. Thus, Lightning could allow any number of transactions without miners' fees.

The Bitcoin community considered this solution. Some miners strongly opposed it, with one group in China leading the resistance. They didn't want to lose their fees. Others thought that Lightning transactions, which are harder to trace than those on the blockchain, would draw a crackdown from the Chinese government. The Chinese government opposed any transaction it couldn't monitor.

In May 2017, more than fifty Bitcoin companies across the globe, including cryptocoin businesses, exchanges, vendors, and service providers, came together to try to resolve the impasse. They drafted a document called the New York Agreement, in which they agreed to work together to improve technology, communication, and coordination to increase the capacity of blockchain to support a higher volume of Bitcoin transactions.

Through this agreement, the volume of Bitcoin transactions doubled. However, another group sought an even higher threshold. On August 1 a new cryptocurrency was introduced: Bitcoin Cash. This currency represented a hard fork from Bitcoin, and thus the two currencies were mutually incompatible. Worse, the agreement to increase Bitcoin's capacity ultimately collapsed in November 2017 when a necessary consensus could not be met.

To some observers, the angry debate, the inability to agree, and the chaotic proposed solutions proved that cryptocurrencies were too unstable and unmanageable. But others concluded just the opposite. Bitcoin and the blockchain ledger had proven to be enduring. It couldn't be changed, even by powerful participants with significant resources.

CHAPTER 4

CRYPTO WINTER

As cryptocurrency prices rose, more financial experts and economists attacked the very notion of a cryptocurrency. Economist and Nobel laureate Paul Krugman said that, contrary to what many seemed to believe, Bitcoin represented not the future of money but a three-hundred-year step backward. "Cryptocurrencies have no backstop, no tether to reality," he wrote. "If speculators were to have a collective moment of doubt, suddenly fearing that Bitcoins were worthless, well, Bitcoins would become worthless."

Paul Krugman's prediction that Bitcoins are susceptible to the same trust issues as those that afflict fiat currencies seemed to come to pass during the so-called crypto winter.

Others noted that investors had given cryptocurrencies two tasks that were impossible to accomplish at the same time. On one hand, speculators were hoping cryptocurrencies would gain value as they attracted attention. On the other, cryptocurrencies were supposed to be a medium of exchange that could buy pizza, a sweater, and a car. But people wouldn't make small purchases such as these using their very valuable cryptocurrency balances. As financial journalist Dan McCrum observed, "No one uses gold bars from the safe for petty cash."

Legendary investor and billionaire Warren Buffett dismissed cryptocurrencies as "rat poison squared," and his partner Charlie Munger added that cryptocurrency trading was "just dementia."

Crypto investor Marc Andreessen gave a sharp response: "I think rich, old white men crapping on technology that they don't understand can be counted on to be wrong roughly 100 percent of the time."

As if to prove the critics right, Bitcoin prices began to fall in early 2018 and then entered a rout. By spring the price had plunged from a high near $20,000 to below $7,500. By the end of the year, it had sunk below $4,000. While Bitcoin had still delivered extraordinary returns for those who had gotten in early, many investors who joined in 2017 were left whiplashed. Most investors who snapped up ICOs ended up with catastrophic losses.

Columnist Lionel Laurent saw the drop in cryptocurrencies as a revolt of sorts against an elitist project. "It marks the general public's resistance to the ideological techno-utopia promised by Bitcoin evangelists. The decentralization they promise remains a niche, even elite, pursuit," he wrote.

During the crypto winter, Bitcoin values fell as much as 80 percent from their previous peak.

"Blockchain became a solution for everything—blockchain for journalism, for [marijuana], for dentists," *New York Times* journalist Nellie Bowles observed. "At the kernel of it all was real technological progress and a growing understanding that this decentralized technology could transform financial systems. But the excitement spun out of control."

As cryptocurrencies crashed and critics pounced, a new phrase circulated among investors: "crypto winter." By March 2019, Bitcoin had dropped about 80 percent from its $19,800 peak in December 2017. Ether had fallen from a high of $1,400 in January 2018 to just $130 a year later. The market value of cryptocurrencies together was down about 85 percent. Initial coin offerings in 2018 raised $12 billion, but in the first three months of 2019, that number was a meager $177 million.

The naysayers had waited for this moment and did not pull punches. "If the crypto faithful devoted as much energy to real innovation," one newspaper columnist quipped, "who knows where we might be as a civilization by now."

Remember cryptokitties, the lovable cat images that were unique and commanded hefty prices? The median price of a unique image reached $41 in March 2018 but had dropped closer to $5 by summer. The transaction volume declined from 1.3 million in December to 115,000 in May. A year later, the site attracted just a few hundred users a day. The cryptokitty named Dragon remained for sale—for about $160,000 in Ether—but couldn't find a buyer.

A *New York Times* reporter went to South Korea to report on the dirty spoons who had dreamed of escaping their situation through cryptocurrencies. Les Mis still owned his Rolls Royce, but many others had lost vast fortunes and were ashamed to tell those closest to them. One cryptocurrency user, Kim Ki-Won, had made enough to quit his job and spend $1,000 each month on "whatever he wanted." Kim hunched over when he discussed losing tens of thousands of dollars, but he was also defiant: "I have nothing to lose. I have always wanted to be rich."

LUNCH WITH BUFFETT

Every year, Warren Buffett auctions off the opportunity to have lunch with him. Businesspeople, investors, and portfolio managers eagerly bid for

Warren Buffett is the fourth-wealthiest person in the world with a net worth of $88.9 billion.

the opportunity to sit with the legendary investor and genius to pitch him their ideas. The winning bid is donated to charity.

In 2019 the winning bid was a shock. Justin Sun, the founder of cryptocurrency TRON, won the lunch for $4.6 million. The surprise came because Buffett had sharply criticized cryptocurrency trading. The twenty-eight-year old Sun, however, was thrilled, calling it a "big win" for blockchain. "I'm excited to talk to Warren Buffett about the promise of blockchain and to get valuable tips from him on entrepreneurship and making bold bets on the future," Sun stated. They had their lunch in January 2020.

Even the most die-hard supporters of cryptocurrencies admitted the environment was grim. Confident talk about disrupting the global financial system was replaced by a more pragmatic focus on survival. "The markets can stay irrational longer than you can stay solvent," says an old investing adage. For cryptocurrency investors, the goal was to avoid going out of business before the next upswing came.

And that upswing had always come. Cryptocurrencies, after all, had been volatile. Some cryptocurrency supporters insisted the latest declines were part of a natural evolution. "It's painful to lose money, but it's a necessary step," said investor Robert Neivert. "2018 was about moving hype to product."

Some noted that at least lawyers were still getting rich. As assets crashed, angry investors turned to the courts. "Now that the market dropped," said a law student, "everyone is getting sued."

The *Financial Times* spotted documents related to a failed ICO on eBay. The reporter called up the founder of the failed coin offering, a young man barely into his twenties, and asked him what happened. "We hired a lawyer and that was a big mistake for us," the founder said. "Because our lawyer basically told us that we should not launch any ICO before we built a real product that might have some users. And I asked him why, because I saw so many ICOs out there who did not have any idea for any product, yet they managed to raise tens of millions of dollars."

The reporter called this a summary of "all that was wrong with the Great Crypto Bubble of 2017–2018."

Falling prices weren't the only problem Bitcoin faced. One company, Bitwise Asset Management, studied all the Bitcoin trades that occurred over a four-day period in March 2019. It used computer analysis to determine which had been completed by real human traders rather than computer-driven programs. Bitwise discovered that of nearly $6 billion in reported trades, only $273 million was legitimate. This study added to skepticism that investors were actually trading Bitcoin—that is, that large amounts of Bitcoin were changing hands each day. Some exchanges, it appeared, were trying to inflate their numbers to get a higher ranking on data services that would then attract other cryptocurrencies to list there. The more cryptocurrencies an exchange offered, the more it received in listing fees and, ultimately, in trading.

Over the years, crypto communities had developed phrases and slang among themselves. As Bitcoin prices fell, crypto supporters comforted and urged one another to "HODL." The term supposedly originated from a crypto supporter in a forum who, in a bout of bad typing or out of drunkenness, posted "I AM HODLING." The phrase evolved into a shorthand for holders determined to keep their cryptocurrencies for the long term despite short-term volatility and crushing losses. They rejected "FUD"—fear, uncertainty, and doubt.

"If you TRULY believe in #bitcoin and #crypto currency, today's price

. . . AND TAXES

In the never-ending argument about fiat currency versus cryptocurrencies, defenders of fiat currency point out it will always have worth because citizens normally pay taxes in their government's money. In addition, the government then uses those funds to pay for public services. However, in November 2018, the State of Ohio became the first to accept Bitcoin for tax payments (though the tax bill was still in US dollars), setting a precedent for other states to follow.

is nothing but a distraction," said a tweet in late November 2018.

As Bitcoin dropped in value, it became less profitable to mine. Miners began to drop out. By the end of 2018, one hundred thousand miners had quit, and 1.4 million computer servers that mined for cryptocurrencies shut down. A measure of the computer power devoted to mining peaked in mid-2018 and then fell by almost half.

Through it all, crypto supporters did not lose the sense they are founding a new world. One wondered what would happen if a bomb went off and killed everyone at a crypto meeting.

"A bomb would set back civilization for years," another said solemnly.

If there was any consolation for crypto supporters, it was that venture capitalists, who invest money early in new products and technologies, had not abandoned blockchain. In fact, venture capitalists invested four times more money in 2018 in blockchain companies than they did in 2017. But cryptocurrencies attracted less desirable attention as well. As interest in cryptocurrencies grew, so did the number of thieves and hackers who saw opportunities to enrich themselves.

CHAPTER 5

HACKS, THIEVES, AND CRITICS

In the decade since Bitcoin was created, at least $15 billion worth of cryptocurrency has been stolen. This number could be even larger, as some thefts go unreported. Since 2017 alone, crypto thieves have made off with nearly $2 billion. These attacks have become increasingly sophisticated and organized. They take advantage of popular misperceptions of what makes a blockchain secure and supposedly unhackable. Like every security system invented, blockchain has both strengths and weaknesses.

MT. GOX HACK

Many security breaches occur not in the cryptocurrencies themselves but in the exchanges on which they are stored. Exchanges are like a combination of banks and marketplaces: they connect buyers and sellers and hold assets—in this case, cryptocurrencies—in accounts. These accounts differ from the private keys associated with blockchain because they are connected to individuals. As a result, cryptocurrency exchanges contain sensitive information about account holders and, most importantly, the holders' cryptocurrency keys.

At its peak in 2013, Mt. Gox was the largest Bitcoin exchange in the world. The exchange had been built by Mark Karpelès, a French-born computer programmer who had settled in Tokyo. As the price of Bitcoin soared, Karpelès appeared to revel in his wealth. He donated 5,000 Bitcoins to the Bitcoin Foundation, an organization dedicated to developing Bitcoin software, and joined its board. Employees reported that he would suddenly approve $400 lunches for the staff or interrupt business to order flat screen TVs for the exchange's Tokyo headquarters.

Mark Karpelès, former CEO of Mt. Gox, was convicted by Japanese courts in March 2019 of falsifying Mt. Gox's financial data.

Mt. Gox's apparent success proved to be a facade. In truth, Mt. Gox had been hacked in 2011, and thieves had gained access to private keys throughout the exchange. Over four years, they stole some 850,000 coins from online wallets. In February 2014, the exchange collapsed into bankruptcy. More than $400 million vanished. Investors around the world lost money, and investor confidence in cryptocurrencies suffered another severe blow.

If there was a moral to the Mt. Gox debacle, according to *Wired* reporter Robert McMillan, it was the need for cryptocurrencies to operate in the real world. "[Cryptocurrency is] a technology that was pushed forward by a community of people who were unprepared or unwilling to deal with even the basics of everyday business," he wrote.

Other investors drew a different moral. Some swore to find the thieves and to bring them to justice. Daniel Kelman, an American lawyer who lived in Taiwan, lost 44.5 Bitcoins, which, at their peak, were worth about $400,000. He connected with Kim Nilsson, a Swedish software engineer who lived in Tokyo. Nilsson was enthusiastic about the potential and promise of cryptocurrencies. He started buying cryptocurrencies in 2012 and opened an account on the Mt. Gox exchange a year later.

Sitting in front of his computer in a cramped Tokyo apartment, Nilsson went to work. The thieves had withdrawn the coins from the exchange over several years. Nilsson was able to search through transactions and detect patterns. Though blockchain addresses are anonymous, Nilsson was fortunate in that parts of the Mt. Gox database, including private

CRYPTOCURRENCIES AND LAW ENFORCEMENT

The FBI actively pursues cryptocurrency criminals. And the City of London Police have begun training their officers to recognize crime financed through digital currencies.

The FBI's Cyber Division, established in 2002, deals with various cyber crimes, including hacking and theft.

records of trades, withdrawals, deposits, and user balances, had been leaked onto the internet. Using this data, Nilsson tracked down nearly two million addresses related to the Mt. Gox exchange. Still, Nilsson had no information on who used the addresses or why.

Nilsson then received help from an unexpected source: Karpelès himself. Karpelès wanted to refute charges that he was part of a conspiracy to loot the Mt. Gox exchange. He agreed to meet Nilsson and helped him complete the list of Mt. Gox addresses. With this information, Nilsson tracked some of the stolen Bitcoins as they moved from one wallet on the Mt. Gox exchange to another. One of these transactions had a note with three letters: "WME." Who or what was WME?

Nilsson searched through the internet and found a WME who ran a currency-exchange business in Moscow, Russia. WME, it turned out, had posted public documents related to his claim that he had been cheated by a trading platform. WME clearly hoped his publicity would force the trading platform to come clean. But he made a mistake. One of his complaints included a letter from his lawyer and the emails he had exchanged with the platform. In one exchange, Nilsson spotted the name on an account held by WME: Alexander Vinnik. Nilsson had found the Mt. Gox thief.

Unknown to Nilsson, US investigators were already following Vinnik for using a digital currency exchange to launder money. In July 2017 Vinnik left Russia to vacation in Greece. Local police and US officials surrounded him on a beach and arrested him. He was charged with laundering more than $4 billion through his digital currency exchange, BTC-e, for individuals connected with a number of crimes, including drug trafficking, identity theft, tax refund fraud, and computer hacking. US investigators said Vinnik had also "obtained" funds from Mt. Gox, which he laundered. According to Greek police, Vinnik was "an internationally sought 'mastermind' of a crime organization."

Nilsson was thrilled the thief had been caught. But he didn't get his money back. Mt. Gox is still in bankruptcy proceedings.

THE 51 PERCENT RULE

Alexander Vinnik was arrested in Greece in 2017 for laundering money. In January 2020, Greek courts agreed to send him to France to stand trial. He will also face trial in the United States and then in his home country of Russia, as these are all places that have brought charges against him. Vinnik maintains that he is innocent.

Mt. Gox is a stunning example of what can go wrong when an exchange is hacked. But what other vulnerabilities might cryptocurrencies have?

In early 2019 a hacker seized control of more than half the network supporting the cryptocurrency Ethereum Classic. The hacker then used this control to rewrite the history of transactions making up the blockchain. With this approach, the hacker transferred more than $1 million to himself. To pull off the heist, the thief exploited the structure of blockchain itself—more specifically, the 51 percent rule.

The 51 percent rule refers to the fact that blockchain transactions are verified by nodes. The nodes are decentralized, so they are theoretically independent from one another. However, if any individual or group were able to control more than half the computing power used to verify transactions, they could send a payment to themselves and then rewrite the blockchain history to send the same payment again.

This type of attack had not targeted common cryptocurrencies because it costs an enormous amount of money to achieve a majority of the mining power. However, hundreds of smaller cryptocurrencies may be far more vulnerable to a "51 percent attack."

In mid-2018, a number of lightly held and traded cryptocurrencies experienced 51 percent attacks. Holders of coins including Verge, Monacoin, and Bitcoin Gold suffered an estimated total of $20 million

CRYPTOCURRENCY VIGILANTES

Some individuals have formed their own groups to pursue crypto thieves. The goal is to identify the thieves and bring them to justice.

in losses. That the attack on the more common Ethereum Classic was successful, however, was more disturbing.

THE DAO

As cryptocurrency holders dealt with exchange issues and 51 percent attacks, another disturbing security flaw emerged—smart contract bugs.

In 2016 a venture capital fund that promised investors a secure, transparent way to collectively make investment decisions launched. This decentralized autonomous organization was called the DAO. It sold tokens that participants could use to direct projects on the Ethereum blockchain.

The DAO was the brainchild of Christoph Jentzsch, a German software developer. Jentzsch pondered how to fund a company. Most companies at the time were simply issuing digital currencies, but Jentzsch thought deeper. Why not create a platform with its own currency to fund a number of start-up projects?

Jentzsch planned to fund developments on the Ethereum blockchain by issuing tokens in exchange for Ether. Investors would then use the tokens to vote for the projects they believed had the most merit. If the app made a return, then it would be distributed back to the token holders. The structure was open and transparent. The owners could watch the money come in, see what was voted on, and how the tokens were allocated.

On April 30, 2016, the DAO was launched with a twenty-eight-day funding window. Jentzsch hoped to raise $5 million for the DAO, but through crowdfunding, investors sent in $150 million. The publicity generated interest in Ether, which drove up demand for the coin. The DAO fund soon reached $250 million, an astonishing amount in such a short time.

"Our hope was it would be the center of a decentralized sharing economy," said Jentzsch later. "For such a big experiment, it was way too early."

A hacker found a flaw in a single letter—a capital *T* should have been lowercase—in line 666 within the smart contract. Through this loophole, the hacker wrote a contract to interact with the DAO. It started siphoning off $4,000 worth of Ether every few minutes and sending it to an address: 0xF35e2cC8E6523d683eD44870f5B7cC785051a77D.

As investors watched helplessly, the DAO was drained of 12 million Ether, equivalent to more than $50 million. After six hours, the hacker stopped.

Jentzsch, frantic to save the remaining funds in the DAO, rallied the Robin Hood Group, a group of Ether experts and computer programmers from around the world to steal the remaining Ether before the hacker could and give it back to the original owners. But as they initiated contracts to save Ether, the original flaw remained, and the hacker continued to exploit it.

The hack showed that the strength of blockchain and smart contracts—that nothing could be altered—could also be a weakness. "Because transactions on a blockchain cannot be undone, deploying a smart contract is a bit like launching a rocket," says Petar Tsankov, a research scientist at ETH Zürich and cofounder of a smart contract security start-up called ChainSecurity. "The software cannot make a mistake."

Some argued that it was not the thieves but the DAO programmers' carelessness that was to blame. The programmers had made a mistake and then they had to pay for it. The programmers, however, were determined to retrieve the money for DAO's shareholders. They argued the heist could prove fatal to the whole idea of blockchain because it was still barely established. And so they proposed a hard fork. The hard fork makes changes that retroactively apply across the blockchain. In effect, the past can literally be rewritten. In block 1,920,000, the programmers wrote code that applied new smart contracts to the Ether coins. DAO investors would be able to get their money back.

Most of the Ethereum community (89 percent) agreed to the hard fork, but a small group (the remaining 11 percent) rejected the solution. They believed that blockchains couldn't simply be rewritten to save individual users. In their view, this could create more problems than it solved, since anyone could come to expect a bailout when things went wrong. In the real world, real people lose real money all the time. It shouldn't be any different for cryptocurrencies and blockchains.

Vitalik Buterin, who helped found Ethereum, waded into the debate in support of the hard fork. "Some Bitcoin users see the hard fork as in some ways violating their most fundamental values," he said. "I personally think these fundamental values, pushed to such extremes, are silly."

For cryptocurrency advocates, the hard fork showed that blockchains themselves didn't represent the freedom their founders had claimed: a decentralized, foolproof system beyond any individual's or government's authority. "The fact that Ethereum could be rolled back means that all blockchains smaller than Bitcoin's are essentially centralized databases under the control of their operators," wrote Saifedean Ammous, author of *The Bitcoin Standard*.

The dispute led to two parallel blockchains: Ethereum and Ethereum Classic. In Ethereum the money was returned to the investors. In Ethereum Classic, the thief retained the stolen DAO tokens.

The DAO attack challenged the confidence of blockchain supporters. But some argued this was to be expected. It was *normal* even. Blockchain supporters pointed to the chaos in the financial system in 2008. Was that any worse? They noted the endless series of trading scandals in which individuals manipulated markets and brought financial firms to collapse. Concentrations of money and wealth always attracted thieves.

In these inevitable stumbles, therefore, they saw hope. Whenever new, innovative systems launch, mistakes happen. The launch of the internet was accompanied by endless criticism claiming it would never take off, that security or some other issue would be insurmountable. But these challenges attracted the resources and intelligence to solve them. Blockchain, in the eyes of its supporters, was the same.

The market rendered its own verdict. Ethereum traded around $10 in the nine months after the attack. Then it joined other cryptocurrencies in soaring to a peak of more than $1,250 in early 2018. Then cryptocurrencies crashed, and Ether dropped to about $100. As of May 2019, it traded at around $230. Ethereum Classic traded at about $7.

In December 2018, as news spread about the vulnerability of cryptocurrencies to hacks and theft, another disturbing event took place. Gerald Cotten, the cofounder and CEO of cryptocurrency exchange QuadrigaCX, reportedly died in India due to complications related to Crohn's disease. Cotten was thirty years old. Cotten's widow, Jennifer Robertson, shocked Quadriga's 115,000 users by claiming the cryptocurrencies on the exchange—worth about $137 million—were inaccessible in offshore accounts. The accounts were only accessible through Cotten's laptop and only Cotten knew the passwords.

On February 5, 2019, the company went bankrupt. An auditor gained access to the digital wallets supposedly holding the cryptocurrencies and found nothing. All digital cash had been pulled from the wallets in 2018. Some accounts were found to be fake.

As more than one hundred thousand Quadriga users wondered whether they would ever see their money again, dozens of conspiracy theories about Cotten crisscrossed the internet. One guessed he had faked his death and was in hiding. Another said he had died, but Quadriga had always been a giant Ponzi scheme.

In this graphic, a fraudulent cryptocurrency exchange (*red*) has received funds from new investors (*blue*) and uses that money to pay itself and its earlier investors (*black*). The earlier investors do not suspect that they have been tricked, but the new investors won't see a return on their investment until even newer investors come along. This kind of fraud is called a Ponzi scheme.

For investors looking for reasons not to trust cryptocurrencies, the case offered plenty. Most disturbing, however, was a smaller detail in the firm's history. In June 2017, according to the *Wall Street Journal,* the firm had upgraded its software and lost 67,000 Ether in a "wallet it couldn't access." The loss at the time was worth $14 million, and the exchange promised it would compensate affected customers. However, because of the appreciation of Ether in the meantime, the loss had ballooned to $90 million. If a glitch in a software update could make money disappear, then perhaps cryptocurrencies were less secure than their supporters claimed.

THE CHALLENGES OF BLOCKCHAIN

Blockchain had often been dismissed by people with little understanding of how it worked. But as the debacles mounted, more informed criticism appeared.

Cybersecurity expert Bruce Schneier noted that if blockchain supporters wanted it to compete with governments and banks, then many people had to trust technology over institutions. As the global financial crisis of 2008–2009 proved—and history provided many more examples—institutions fail. But technology, and the people who use it, can also fail. In fact, Schneier listed a number of ways that users could lose their blockchain-based cryptocurrencies.

"If your Bitcoin exchange gets hacked, you lose all of your money," stated Schneier. "If your Bitcoin wallet gets hacked, you lose all of your money. If you forget your login credentials, you lose all of your money. If there's a bug in the code of your smart contract, you lose all of your money. If someone successfully hacks the blockchain security, you lose all of your money."

In response, several companies formed to address the security threats to blockchains. One of the most common approaches was the most intuitive: subject smart contracts to rigorous audits before they're launched. These audits should be able to find most coding errors and bugs that can lead to security breaches. Others developed smart contracts known as bug bounties. If an individual finds a bug and reports it, they receive a reward.

But these solutions, so far, seem complicated, expensive, time-consuming, and limited. Smart contracts are, after all, in their infancy. They are also up against a system that has developed over millions of years: human nature. As Bloomberg columnist Noah Smith summed it up, "All the techno-wizardry of blockchains can't overcome the power of good old human dishonesty."

Other critics, however, focused on blockchain technology itself being inherently flawed and therefore not useful—especially compared to the potential that cryptocurrency supporters claimed it had.

In a blog post, tech veteran Kai Stinchcombe noted that blockchain had attracted interest and supposed investment from large, creditable companies. But, he said, these "corporate boosters" had "gone long on press and short on actual rollout." He pointed out that blockchain company Ripple—whose head at one time was worth more than Facebook's founder, Mark Zuckerberg—did not use blockchain itself. "You read that right," he wrote in the blog post. "The company Ripple decided the best way to move money across international borders was to not use Ripples."

Stinchcombe's criticism was fairly simple. Blockchain, it turned out, could not be successfully applied to real-world problems. In 2006, he noted, Walmart tried to track the movement of individual bananas and mangoes from trees on a farm to shelves in a store. The effort failed because of the difficulty in getting everyone on the supply chain to enter data. A decade later, Walmart tried again, this time using blockchain. To Stinchcombe, the very framing of the problem and solution was absurd. If mango pickers did not like to enter produce information into a data tracking system, the solution was not "let's create a very long sequence of small files, each one containing a hash of the previous file."

"People treat blockchain as a 'futuristic integrity wand,'" wrote Stinchcombe. "Wave a blockchain at the problem, and suddenly your data will be valid. For almost anything people want to be *valid*, blockchain has been proposed as a solution."

The reality, Stinchcombe concluded, was that no one had actually used blockchain as a solution. "There *is no single person in existence* who had a problem they wanted to solve, discovered that an available blockchain solution was the best way to solve it, and therefore became a blockchain enthusiast."

Stinchcombe pointed out the elephant in the room: How was the average person to know if a smart contract—written in computer code—could be trusted? You must read through it. This could take a couple of hours. Stinchcombe gave the example of buying an e-book. Say you bought a book directly from a novelist, and the smart contract arrived on your computer. The contract should state how much money will be withdrawn from your account for the delivery of the book. Reading through the contract to make sure there aren't any bugs or errors would take far more time and effort than the e-book is worth.

"Auditing software is hard!" wrote Stinchcombe. "The most-heavily scrutinized smart contract in history had a small bug that nobody noticed—that is, until someone did notice it, and used it to steal fifty million dollars. If cryptocurrency enthusiasts putting together a

[$150 million] investment fund can't properly audit the software, how confident are you in your e-book audit? Perhaps you would rather write your own counteroffer software contract, in case this e-book author has hidden a recursion bug in their version to drain your Ethereum wallet of all your life savings?"

The point, said Stinchcombe, is that blockchain was not trustless—it simply asks people to trust technology rather than other people. This makes some sense—after all, we trust technology to conduct vital tasks all the time. But in reality, we're actually trusting a third party to verify that the technology can be trusted. Blockchain, therefore, puts the task of verifying trust back on to the individual. This requires extraordinary knowledge, resources, and time. And this, according to Stinchcombe, makes blockchain far less effective than its supporters claim.

Financial Times journalist Dan McCrum used Stinchcombe's argument to make a startling conclusion: "Blockchain doesn't even solve most problems of trust. The integrity of data on a public blockchain can be trusted not to change, but that says nothing about whether the data is right in the first place. For votes, tuna, shipping containers, or mango supply chains, a blockchain registry would only be as good or as trustworthy as the people contributing to it."

Finally, there was another painful reality about blockchain. Even by mid-2019, few average internet users were actually using it. Blockchain enthusiasts envisioned Dapps functioning as apps on an iPhone. Because Dapps were outside the control of giant tech companies, they offered users a way to bypass gatekeepers and avoid the incessant tracking that occurs on the internet. Of the twenty-seven hundred Dapps with enough data for statistical measurement, however, only three attracted more than ten thousand daily users. In fact, thirty of the top fifty Dapps were dedicated to gambling.

One problem with Dapps is that users have to get used to a whole new blockchain-based operating system. In comparison, downloading an app

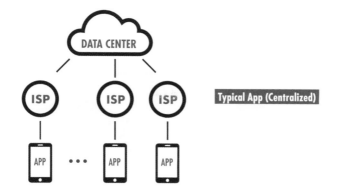

Typical App (Centralized)

Decentralized App (Dapp)

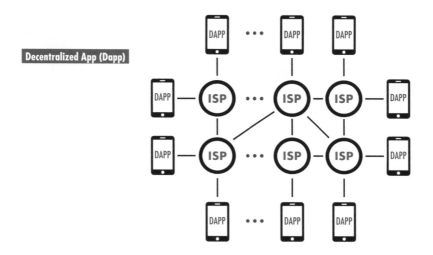

The smartphone apps you might be used to rely on a centralized data center to deliver content to your phone through an internet service provider (ISP). A Dapp relies on a decentralized method, where users are connected to one another rather than to a single entity, to deliver content.

onto a smartphone is relatively simple and easy. Blockchain's operating system remains in a relatively early phase. Programmers are building and troubleshooting the system. User experience is not yet a focus.

"Does it run? Yeah, it runs, like if I built a car," said one computer science professor. "It'll run, but it's not something you'd want to put your kids in."

CHAPTER 6

BLOCKCHAIN: THE TULIP BULB OF THE INTERNET?

Where is blockchain today, and where is it going? To its critics, blockchain is little more than a speculative bubble—another power grab by technologists, a solution in search of a problem, and a system rife with errors. It's vulnerable to thieves and hacks, or otherwise hopelessly compromised. But to its supporters, blockchain represents nothing less than a revolution. It establishes what makes human affairs work: truth, which leads to trust. It takes control of the internet back from the tech companies, gatekeepers, and totalitarian governments. In their eyes, the challenges and missteps of the past decade are to be expected given the enormity of blockchain's potential.

The infrastructure to fully support cryptocurrencies is coming into place. Several exchanges—such as Binance HK, Upbit, and Huobi—have set up digital currency ventures. Miners operate all over the world. Supply chains, including those of Walmart, are adopting blockchain technology. In May 2019, companies such as Amazon, Whole Foods, Nordstrom, AT&T, and Barnes and Noble began accepting cryptocurrency for payments.

However, there have also been stumbles. The 2018 crash in Bitcoin and other cryptocurrencies weakened investor demand and interest. The volatility of their value made cryptocurrencies difficult to use as a medium of exchange. Major Wall Street institutions such as Goldman Sachs and the Chicago Board Options Exchange delayed, or dropped, plans to offer trading support for Bitcoin.

"When you talk to tech industry insiders about where [blockchain] is heading, two vastly different comparisons are inevitable: the tulip bulb and the internet," observed a *New York Times* reporter. The tulip bulb craze occurred in the seventeenth century in the Netherlands, when speculators bid up the price of tulip flower bulbs on newly opened markets. The prices reached astronomical levels and then abruptly collapsed, and the tulip craze has become shorthand for speculative bubbles. The internet, on the other hand, was also a speculative bubble that popped in 2000. But it ultimately rewarded investors. "So what is it?" asks the article. "We are still a few years from any sort of clarity about where this technology will fit in the world."

RESTORING TRUST IN DATA

According to its supporters, one of the biggest potential applications of blockchain is data. All around us, networked appliances, vehicles, laptop and desktop computers and, of course, smartphones, are talking to the network. They share information—billions of bits of data. Analysts and programs sift through this vast trove to glean insights. Imagine if doctors could track the spread of disease with extraordinary accuracy in real time. Or if machine parts informed users when they need to be replaced. Or if the progress of a customized educational program could be confirmed in real time.

Data can provide vital clues to consumer behavior, voter preferences, and organizational effectiveness. We often think of Amazon as a website where we can buy virtually anything and have it shipped directly to us. In reality, Amazon is as much a data-gathering company that holds valuable information on its customers' shopping habits. Other companies such as Google, Facebook, and Apple have similar pools of user data. These companies protectively guard their data. Their high stock prices are evidence of their commanding position in the economy.

However, public trust in these companies has fallen in recent years. It was revealed that consumer data has been used to manipulate, spy on, and target and deliver "fake news" to users. Many users now wonder how their data is being used—or abused. Trust is a critical component for all transactions, and trust in the era of data collection is near all-time lows.

Many companies do not abuse the data they collect but have shown they can't be trusted to protect it. Because user data is so valuable, these companies have been targeted by hackers. Every few months, it seems, another company reports a significant data breach. A hack of Twitter data, for example, led to email in-boxes jammed with spam, sophisticated scam campaigns, and harassment.

Finally, many people have privacy concerns. They don't want their data to be recorded, analyzed, shared, or possibly stolen. They don't want a third party to use it to push an ad telling them what to buy. They don't want to be manipulated by targeted media stories telling them what to think and who to vote for. Long after a person searches for or even purchases an item, ads for it can appear in their browser. It is an annoying and sometimes unsettling reminder that we're always being watched.

How can the promise of data be realized with these severe limitations? How can trust be restored? According to some, the answer is blockchain.

Billions of transactions occur every day on the internet. These transactions are recorded through third parties, who can use, abuse, or lose the data. The third parties can analyze the data for their own purposes or sell it to another party without their users' knowledge. Moreover, whoever holds the data can combine it with other data about the user, forming a more complete (or distorted) image of them.

Blockchain removes the intermediary, limiting the exchange of data to the two parties. The exchange can be made in private and is confined specifically to the transaction. This means a user can buy something without allowing third parties to track them all over the internet. Blockchain also allows users to take control of their data. Without blockchain, users typically log into a website with a specific ID name that is verified with a password. The user may think they own this experience. After all, it's their name, password, and data. However, everything—the user's identity and content—is actually hosted by the website.

"Apps were not responsive to customers so much as designed to lock them in," said tech company founder Ryan Shea. "You go into the net and Facebook or Google or Dropbox or Pinterest or Amazon all want you to move in, giving them all your documents, music, providing storage for your life. Medical sites want to store all your health data. You have to petition to get it when you want it."

In an era of ever-rising concern about data and privacy, as well as the potential for hyperefficient internet giants to shape societies and economies in ways that benefit them, blockchain may become a potent alternative. Decentralized, private blockchain addresses provide an alternative to the current, tedious system in which each website requires a separate ID and password. The individual retains control over their identity and data rather than handing them off to an app or platform.

To understand how this might work in the future, consider the following example: you are on a long drive in your electric vehicle and need to charge up. However, no charging stations are nearby. You instead pull up to a house that has advertised itself as a charging station for electric cars. You plug in and authorize payment via blockchain, using a digital currency from your digital wallet. The exchange is made, and you're back on the road.

This transaction may seem fairly simple, but it requires a lot of trust. A blockchain must verify that the car is owned by the driver, that they have the money to pay, and that they are not using software that may infect the homeowner's computers with a virus. Without blockchain technology, there are a number of different gatekeepers that could slow down, or even prevent, the transaction. The electrical company could sell its electricity only to individuals within a certain jurisdiction. The car company may negotiate to have its cars only serviced at specific charging stations. The telecom company may not allow the transaction unless it's paid a special fee. And the current financial system—where exchanges of cash and securities are expensive and can literally take days to settle—is not going to enable a quick exchange of digital currency.

With blockchain, all of this is bypassed. The individual owns their identity, their money, and their things (in this case, a car). They carry out a transaction with another individual without a third party or intermediary. They do not need a government or financial institution. They do not even need a prior relationship or reputation to establish trust. It is easy to understand why totalitarian regimes and police states are regarding cryptocurrencies with suspicion and, in some cases, outright banning them. In the example described above, blockchain is an enabler of freedom.

ESTABLISHING THE PERSON

Part of freedom is having the right to self-determination, to control your own identity. In many societies, people do not have access to their own pasts or to their own selves. They may have lived in a home or on a piece of land for decades and yet have no proof they own it. They may have skills or characteristics but no way to verify them to a government or a bank. Millions of people live in these precarious circumstances all over the world.

In other places, people have records—birth certificates, passports, driver's licenses, deeds of ownership, credit histories, and so on—that can be used to prove to the government and other institutions they are who they say they are and own what they say they own. Because individuals can establish their identities, they are able to take out loans, take advantage of financial and educational opportunities, and invest in themselves. They can access short-term credit cards for emergencies and long-term loans to finance home purchases or their educations. Individuals outside of this system—who are generally poorer—actually have to pay more for services such as banking and are locked out of making money off their assets.

In Manila, Philippines, more than five hundred thousand squatters live in structures with no titles to the land they live on. This leaves them vulnerable to challenges from the government and private landowners. In Brazil, millions live in vast favelas—neighborhoods of shacks and homes built by people on land they do not own. In countries in South Asia, such as India, rural farmers cultivate crops on public land. Without titles (deeds) to the property they work on, these people are deprived of their investments, any improvements they have made to the property, and any savings. They lose their past and are denied their future.

A serious problem is that record keepers in many societies are incompetent and corrupt. An individual may try to get a deed to a piece of land—its exact location, the dates when it was bought and sold—and find the records are out of order, or improperly entered. Or someone could bribe an official to write a different name on the deed, effectively stealing the title of ownership. In the United States and Canada, Native Americans have been forced to give up their land under threat of violence, and the federal governments have failed to honor treaties and laws signed regarding Native land rights and ownership. This corruption favors the wealthy and powerful.

"Governments have been known to make up completely new land registries and say, 'Hey, this land is ours and nobody lives here,'" noted conservation biologist Guillaume Chapron. This is especially common if natural resources are present in the area.

Blockchain could be a solution to these challenges. Because of the decentralized ledger accounting system, blockchain contracts can't be altered. They are transparent and universally accessible to anyone with access to the internet. This impacts more than online shopping. Blockchain could allow billions of people access to the modern global economy—people who have previously been ignored, exploited, or simply left out.

"The time stamp makes this all possible," noted authors Michael Casey and Paul Vigna, "because it inserts a declaration that a milestone has occurred—a birth, a graduation, a property transfer, a marriage—into a commonly accepted record of history to which all can refer."

Individuals who own their own homes, for example, are typically better stewards of it. They often participate more in local government and seek solutions to common problems. They become active citizens in a world where active citizenship is more needed than ever.

But again, a decentralized ledger doesn't guarantee that the original coding is valid. It could have been written incorrectly or deliberately corrupted. Users must always read the fine print—whether it's computer code or the end of a contract. Blind faith in blockchain is not a solution. Blockchain by itself cannot overcome tyranny, build social cohesion, eliminate corruption, or otherwise ward off the many challenges people face.

Headquarted in New York City, JPMorgan is the largest bank in the United States. It has only recently begun investing in cryptocurrencies.

BLOCKCHAIN AND BANKING

Banks have naturally been skeptical about a system that blockchain enthusiasts claim will replace them. One wealthy investor stated that he bought Bitcoin to "support a way of ripping apart the financial system." Recently, however, banks have started to embrace the new technology. Many have released coins that are guaranteed by the US dollar or other assets, thus helping to avoid the wild swings cryptocurrencies have experienced in the past. One cryptocurrency, Utility Settlement Coin, allows banks to move money among themselves more efficiently.

JPMorgan CEO Jamie Dimon, who once threatened to fire employees if they traded Bitcoin, announced that JPMorgan would introduce its own digital token, a first for a major US bank. Despite calling Bitcoin a "fraud," Dimon came around to recognize blockchain's potential.

JPMorgan, after all, had already developed Quorum, a blockchain platform that companies used to track financial data.

According to the bank, clients had asked for a way to move their money onto blockchain. Securities are typically bought, sold, and delivered (or settled) through the Depository Trust and Clearing Corporation, an institution jointly owned by banks. The steps to ensure the secure and legal transfer of a security are numerous, tedious, time-consuming, and costly. About $50 billion of trades fail each day in the US Treasury market, representing a significant loss and friction for the markets.

These failures are also expensive for the banks. The attraction, said JPMorgan's head of blockchain, was that large institutions wanted to move money safely and, above all, quickly. Through Quorum, the institution's money is converted to JPM Coins, which are backed by US dollars. Once the transaction is completed, the JPM Coins are converted back into US dollars. This allows institutions to bypass the relatively laborious process of wiring money.

In China, the world's second-largest economy, financial regulators have taken a deep interest in blockchain. The Communist Party of China, which rules the country, has moved to prevent cryptocurrencies from operating outside government control. China has banned cryptocurrency exchanges and ICOs. Instead, the People's Bank of China (PBOC) has reportedly begun developing a digital currency to replace cash. Though details haven't been confirmed, Chinese citizens may be given digital wallets in exchange for their cash. This would allow the PBOC to track virtually all its citizens' transactions, as all purchases would occur digitally. This system is at odds with the vision of the first cryptocurrency developers.

Banks and cryptocurrencies face other challenges. Financial companies are among the most regulated in the industry. This is for good reason. Irresponsible banking, lending, and speculation have led to asset bubbles, financial panics, and economic devastation, all of which have made populations miserable, overthrown governments, and even brought on war. While blockchain is supposedly transparent, regulators will need time to understand the technology and its implications.

"The standard answer of 'just go to your local Chase branch' doesn't work in crypto," cryptocurrency trader Sam Bankman-Fried told a Bloomberg reporter. "It's not illegal for big banks to bank the crypto industry, but it's a massive compliance headache that they don't want to put the resources in to solve."

How cryptocurrencies will ultimately affect banking is still being worked out. Though banks are already using blockchain to become more efficient, its intended purpose—to replace intermediaries—is still more potential than reality.

BLOCKCHAIN: JOB DESTROYER?

Given the current political and social instability in the United States, blockchain may provide solutions to issues within the labor market.

All effective innovation puts pressure on specific industries and the people who work in them. Blockchain could potentially make record keepers, and the individuals who monitor and ensure they are correct, redundant. Record keeping is not a small industry. More than one million people are classified as accountants in the United States alone. But the change may affect more than just that profession. Wall Street employs—and pays very well—teams of analysts and portfolio managers who wait for earnings releases and quarterly data. Blockchain could make this content available in real time and verify its accuracy—no need to wait around for the information. Banks, too, are huge employers at all stages of the financial process, from making loans to verifying transactions to providing due diligence for customers.

The loss of many high-paying, upper-middle-class professions could be destabilizing. It could make current angry debates about immigrants, foreign competition, and globalization appear tame by comparison.

As more automated machines take over manual labor, and as software based on algorithms replace traditionally white-collar jobs, we are left to ask what kind of world this leaves for human beings. The role of work in our lives, the importance of dignity, the pride of building something on our own—all of this must be discussed, debated, and solved, or those creating the technology will do it for us.

Some believe that humans, once unencumbered by meaningless work, will focus on their own creative potential. The irony is that creative industries, such as music, visual art, and writing, were some of the first professions consumed by technology. Can blockchain be part of the solution?

Technology made it virtually free to copy writing, music, or film, and to reproduce and distribute it. Blockchain, however, solves this problem by establishing something that cannot be reproduced—something unique. Thus, an artist can create something and have it exist as the sole copy (or as one of a number of copies) to be sold and distributed. This is a first step. To create a digital economy that works for individual artists, it is critical to establish the singularity of a work and the person who created it.

BLOCKCHAIN AND DEMOCRACY

Blockchain could also help the relationship between democratic governments and their voters. Some of the biggest challenges in any democracy are voter fraud and voter suppression. Since citizens first held elections, individuals have tampered with the process. Traditionally, individuals would vote several times or add votes to stuff ballot boxes. Notorious in the United States are methods that deny individuals their right to vote through poll taxes, tests, and gerrymandering, or because of infractions on their record. Subtler efforts to influence voting include locating polling stations in remote or difficult-to-access areas.

Technology enthusiasts have long advocated using the internet for voting. An election could be held online, with individuals simply tapping

Just outside of Zürich, Switzerland, the small town of Zug is sometimes called Crypto Valley, a play on the more famous Silicon Valley in California.

their smartphones to register their votes. This would undoubtedly raise voter participation—no more traveling to polling stations, waiting in lines, or navigating cumbersome registration procedures. Online voting could also potentially address the fact that polling devices in the United States are sometimes old, broken, hacked, or ineffective.

Blockchain, which establishes one copy, can theoretically establish one vote. In late June 2018, Zug, a city in Switzerland, held a trial vote using blockchain technology. Zug is part of a group trying to establish itself as a center of blockchain innovation. Zug established an electronic ID system that allowed its citizens to vote through their smartphones on a specific issue. The municipal government claimed the experiment was a success because voters registered their votes easily and anonymously.

Estonia, a European country of 1.3 million on the Baltic Sea, is leading another effort to use blockchain in voting. For several years, the country has transitioned from a traditional government to a fully digital one. Each citizen has been issued a secure ID card. They can vote for candidates on their home computers. They can file taxes, apply for loans, or see a doctor without the paperwork needed in other systems because the information can be accessed online.

The security of this system is based on Keyless Signature Infrastructure (KSI), a blockchain technology. KSI was developed by an Estonian company, Guardtime. The US military is among Guardtime's largest customers.

To understand why blockchain could be so important for security, it's vital to understand why security breaches can be so devastating. In conventional terms, people typically understand a data breach as someone seeing secret information. But that's only part of the problem. The other, perhaps more important, security threat is that someone can alter data without being noticed. The details of your medical records are probably not important to a data thief. But if someone changed those details—for example, the medications you're allergic to—that could be deadly the next time you're at a hospital.

BLOCKCHAIN AND ENERGY

Mining for Bitcoin takes enormous computational power, and those computers consume significant amounts of energy. One estimate was that, by 2015, miners around the world were using more energy than the entire country of Austria. Much of this mining was being done in China, where a majority of power stations were powered by burning coal.

This example can be applied to many other scenarios. Imagine if voting records, tax records and payments, or land titles were changed without anyone being able to track the change. The average time before a data breach is detected is 197 days. That's plenty of time to create havoc with records. The blockchain, however, makes every alteration immediately noticeable, ensuring that the records are sound. More importantly, technologies such as KSI are able to monitor the integrity of information while not having access to the data itself. Thus, information can be kept protected and private.

BLOCKCHAIN AND THE ENVIRONMENT

Blockchain supporters believe that, in addition to supporting democracy, blockchain could be a crucial part of the solution to the most serious challenge we face: the destruction of the natural world.

Blockchain has already been used to track food. This allows consumers to know their food has been responsibly raised, captured, and delivered. Other companies have started piloting blockchain programs that allow individuals to trade their excess energy. In Japan, blockchain enables customer-to-customer relationships by establishing who owns what energy and how much of it is theirs. Ultimately, the goal is to have rural power customers create their own renewable energy sources and then sell their energy over the grid to other customers. The end result is a reduction in carbon emissions.

Blockchain by itself won't save the planet. However, supporters argue, by establishing trust on a vast scale, it can be an enormous tool. It can enable concerned individuals to connect, verify, and trade. It allows people to work together. As the environmental crisis mounts, blockchain supporters argue that it will likely be at the center of the solution—an answer to critics who wondered when blockchain would find a problem.

BLOCKCHAIN IS THE FUTURE?

The innovation inspired by blockchain, and the potential it holds, are still in the opening stages. Will blockchain improve access to technology? Will it contribute to a more level playing field for users? Will it let individuals collaborate more effectively? Or will blockchain lead to yet more centralized control, more alienation, and more abuse from those who hold power?

The most optimistic vision of blockchain is that it can help upend our current technological situation, which seems destined for some kind of dystopian dead end. A few giant companies currently dominate, offering "free" services that are actually paid for with very valuable user data. This data is used by the companies for their own benefit in ways mostly unknown to the general user. The companies also abuse their position to stifle innovation and competition, and ultimately dictate users' online experiences.

"I wouldn't say the internet has failed with a capital *F*, but it has failed to deliver the positive, constructive society many of us had hoped for," noted Sir Tim Berners-Lee, the inventor of the World Wide Web.

Supporters of digital tokens believe they will inspire a new wave of innovation and creativity, especially when building public tools—or open protocols—for use on the internet. In the past, the internet was mostly built by institutions that did not need to serve the needs of stakeholders—i.e., the government, universities, and nonprofits. The individuals who created these tools, for the most part, were not able to directly profit from their labor. Consequently, the top software engineering talent tended to go to companies that could pay the most. Projects for the common good that might not immediately generate revenue, on the other hand, languished. With tokens, however, individuals could now create open protocols that benefit everyone—and get paid for it.

"This ecosystem of tokens and open platforms is starting to look like the map of a new, decentralized economic future," wrote financial journalists Michael Casey and Paul Vigna. "In fact, these digital assets might even become the primary means by which human beings generate and exchange value."

LIBRA

In June 2019 Facebook announced its plans to create a new cryptocurrency, Libra, which would be based on the open-source Libra Blockchain. Facebook's goal was to make Libra available to its more than two billion users, who could use Facebook apps to make and receive payments. The currency would be managed by the Libra Association, a nonprofit based in Switzerland that included companies such as Visa, PayPal, and Uber. Libra would be backed by bank deposits and short-term government securities.

Supporters spoke of the benefits Libra could bring. It would charge virtually no transaction fees—a potential boon for the many people worldwide without a bank account or other access to the financial system. It would bring cryptocurrencies and blockchain technology into the mainstream but remain outside the control of Wall Street and central banks. Facebook executives portrayed it as a new system that would favor users over institutions.

"It feels like it is time for a better system," said David Marcus, head of Facebook's blockchain technology research. "This is something that could be a profound change for the entire world."

Within just a few months, however, Facebook's Libra ran into trouble. Government officials were cool to the project, while regulators criticized it on the basis of Facebook's notorious privacy issues. Others questioned whether tech companies could handle such an enormous responsibility. To them, Libra's creation seemed an act of arrogance.

"I think it is extraordinary how [ignorant] Facebook is about how and why the financial system works," said tech veteran Halsey Minor at a conference. "Nobody wants to hold a currency that is not their

Mark Zuckerberg, founder of Facebook, speaks at a summit on May 1, 2018. He believes Libra could bring cryptocurrencies into the mainstream.

own. There is not one single person out there that is going, 'give me a new currency.'"

Minor compared Facebook to countries such as China, Russia, and Iran, who are seeking a financial system outside the US dollar. Representative Nydia Velázquez of New York noted that a company with the motto "move fast and break things" may not be the best source for a new currency. "Mr. Zuckerberg, we do not want to break the international monetary system," she said.

Zuckerberg himself seemed humbled by the fierce response to Libra. He told the US Congress that management of the currency would be in the hands of an association. Most revealingly, he admitted, "I'm sure people wish it was anyone but Facebook putting this idea forward."

Partners such as MasterCard began to drop out as the backlash grew. Facebook publicly said it might have to delay Libra's launch. A system that developers claimed would establish trust between strangers was facing scrutiny because tech companies had lost the public trust.

Other power brokers in the world, however, noticed Facebook's effort. They were determined not to be left behind. In China, cryptocurrencies had been banned because the central government did not want a financial system to operate outside its control. Chinese president Xi Jinping, however, stated that blockchain was important for the future and that it was vital for China to have a role in its development.

Soon after his remarks were made public, Chinese stocks even loosely related to blockchain rose sharply. In fact, shares in more than seventy companies had to be suspended after they hit their daily limit. The government quickly released a statement that said investors should not drive up stocks in every blockchain-related company.

"The future is here for blockchain, but we need to stay rational," reported the government newspaper, the *People's Daily*.

WHAT ABOUT SATOSHI NAKAMOTO?

As the world caught up to their ideas about cryptocurrencies and blockchain, Satoshi Nakamoto remained mostly silent and hidden. In fact, since December 2011, Nakamoto has essentially disappeared. On March 6, 2014, they sent a simple, five-worded message—"I am not Dorian Nakamoto." This was in reference to a Dorian Satoshi Nakamoto, a former CIA computer coder in Los Angeles who, because of his name, had been hounded by the media as the founder of Bitcoin. That was the real Nakamoto's last public message.

Many have speculated as to why Nakamoto has withdrawn from any kind of public life. The most obvious reason is that Nakamoto could be worth billions of dollars and, as such, a target for criminals. Another is that Nakamoto wants to keep as much focus on their creation, Bitcoin, as possible so that the system becomes more secure and trusted. Finally, however, Nakamoto may fear the collective power of governments, states, and financiers who sit atop the current system based on fiat currency. Given the threat Bitcoin may pose to this system—and the ways it has been useful to non-state actors such as criminals, drug traders, and terrorists—Nakamoto may be wise to keep themselves anonymous.

A few individuals have since emerged to claim the identity of Satoshi Nakamoto. One of the most prominent has been Craig Wright, an Australian computer programmer.

In 2015 *Wired* magazine announced Craig Wright was most likely the mystery individual behind Satoshi Nakamoto. *Wired* reported that it had secretly received leaked information—including emails and a trust agreement—that indicated Wright was Nakamoto. *Wired* published its results, though it also cautioned: "Either Wright invented Bitcoin, or he's a brilliant hoaxer who very badly wants us to believe he did."

How did he come up with the name? Wright told the *Economist* that Tominaga Nakamoto was a seventeenth-century Japanese philosopher, merchant, and freethinker who was very critical of his society.

A few weeks after publishing the story, however, *Wired* indicated some troubling inconsistencies had arisen. Wright, according to *Wired*, had misrepresented his education credentials and had backdated blog posts to make it look as if he had been involved in creating Bitcoin.

Skeptics wondered why Wright, if he were Nakamoto, did not simply produce Nakamoto's private key. Only Nakamoto has it. Moreover, Nakamoto, if they are not Wright, has remained silent. No one has heard from them since their clarification about Dorian Nakamoto.

BORING

Perhaps Nakamoto wanted to be like his cryptocurrency: normal—boring, even. After falling in value by almost 75 percent in 2018, Bitcoin, against

In 2019 Craig Wright, claiming to be Satoshi Nakamoto, sued several people who called him a fraud, including Ethereum founder Vitalik Buterin.

most expectations, began to rise again. The catalyst appeared to be a sudden change in monetary policy from the world's most important central bank: the US Federal Reserve. In January 2019 the Federal Reserve announced it would begin loosening its monetary policy because the economy was weakening and investors had grown nervous.

The new policy typically encouraged investors to buy riskier assets. By the end of May, the price of Bitcoin had more than doubled. Other cryptocurrencies also benefited. That year Litecoin rose 290 percent through May. Ethereum was up 110 percent.

"The crypto winter is gone," said a blockchain and cryptocurrency investor.

Despite cryptocurrencies' decentralized nature, they are connected to the rises and falls of the rest of the economy and of financial institutions such as banks and traditional stock exchanges. In 2018 the operator of the New York Stock Exchange announced it was going to create its own cryptocurrency exchange.

Mike Orcutt, an associate editor at *MIT Technology Review* who focused on blockchain and cryptocurrencies, was more hopeful. "In 2019, blockchains will start to become boring," he wrote. "After the Great Crypto Bull Run of 2017 and the monumental crash of 2018, blockchain technology won't make as much noise in 2019. But it will become more useful."

According to the website 99Bitcoins, the year 2018 saw ninety-three Bitcoin obituaries that claimed the death of the cryptocurrency. It is clear now that writers exaggerated these deaths. Digital currencies are a part of the financial and social landscape. In fact, Bitcoin and blockchain have become almost normal or, as Orcutt's article put it, "boring."

In October 2019 the Peterson Institute for International Economics hosted a seminar that asked a critical question: "What is the future of money in the digital age?"

Economist Martin Wolf noted that one idea in these discussions struck him as particularly interesting. Perhaps digital currencies are a chance for central banks—in other words, the government—to reassert its role in the global economy.

"Just as the internet has ended up as more of a source of enhanced government control than one of greater freedom . . . so the revolution in digital money might allow the central bank to replace the liabilities of private banks with its own," Wolf wrote. "In this way, the seigniorage from money creation, now enjoyed by private banking, would be transferred back to taxpayers."

Cryptocurrencies, once seen as a new, independent form of money outside of centralized control, may in fact be brought under government by a new generation of citizens tired of the abuses of the private market. It is difficult to conceive of a more ironic result from the cryptocurrency revolution.

Timeline

2008	August:	Bitcoin.org is registered.
	October:	"Bitcoin: A Peer-to-Peer Electronic Cash System" is published.
2009	January:	The first block of Bitcoins (the "Genesis Block") is mined.
		Satoshi Nakamoto conducts the first Bitcoin transaction when they send ten Bitcoins to computer programmer Hal Finley.
2010	May:	Laszlo Hanyecz exchanges 10,000 Bitcoin for two pizzas worth twenty-five dollars.
	July:	Bitcoin's value rises above a penny.
		Mt. Gox opens.
2011	January:	The Silk Road Dark Web marketplace launches.
	February:	Bitcoin's value reaches parity with one dollar.
2012	April:	Bitcoin's value rises above $100.
2013	May:	The first Bitcoin ATM starts operating in San Diego, California.
	October:	The Silk Road Dark Web is shut down by the FBI.
	November:	Bitcoin's value rises above $1,000.
		Vitalik Buterin writes the Ethereum white paper.
2014	February:	After years of theft, the Mt. Gox exchange collapses.
2015	July:	The Ethereum network launches.
2016	February:	Bitcoin Classic is launched.
	April:	The DAO launches and is later hacked.

2017	August:	Bitcoin Cash is launched.
	December:	Bitcoin rises above $10,000.
		Bitcoin's value peaks at $19,783.
2018	January:	Bitcoin's price falls to as low as $9,199.59, half its peak price, and then declines to less than $4,000 over the next several months.
	June:	Zug, Switzerland, tests blockchain technology for voting.
	November:	Ohio becomes the first US state to accept Bitcoin for tax payments.
	December:	Gerald Cotten of cryptocurrency exchange QuadrigaCX reportedly dies in India.
2019	January:	Ethereum Classic suffers a 51 percent attack.
	February:	Cryptocurrency exchange QuadrigaCX goes bankrupt.
	May:	Online retailers, including Amazon and Barnes and Noble, begin accepting cryptocurrencies.
	June:	Facebook announces its cryptocurrency, Libra.
		Justin Sun, founder of the cryptocurrency TRON, bids $4.6 million to win lunch with Warren Buffett.
2020	January:	Justin Sun and Warren Buffett have lunch.
2140		The last Bitcoin will be mined.

Glossary

altcoin: a shortened version of "Bitcoin alternative" that applies to the number of digital coins in circulation, many of them forks of Bitcoin with minor changes to the proof of work

block: a file of data recorded on the blockchain network that includes the record of some or all new blockchain transactions. New blocks are secured to the rest of the chain via cryptography, and none can be altered without changing the rest of the chain.

blockchain: a decentralized, digital ledger of records that cannot be changed without the consensus of the majority of participants. Transactions are recorded and time-stamped in "blocks" that are linked together with cryptography.

cryptocurrencies: currencies based on blockchain that use cryptography and a decentralized system to corroborate and verify transactions

Dapp (decentralized application): a decentralized, open-source, autonomous application, with all records stored on a blockchain. It can distribute tokens.

Ethereum: an open-source software platform that uses blockchain technology to enable developers to write smart contracts and build and deploy Dapps

fiat currency: physical money, such as paper bills or coins

fork: the splitting of a blockchain into two simultaneous versions that share blocks. The community decides which version to use, and the discarded version becomes an orphan.

hard fork: a change to the rules of a blockchain that requires all users to adapt to the change

initial coin offering (ICO): crowdfunding through blockchain, with ideas, individuals, and projects looking for support by distributing coins or tokens

intermediary: a person or organization that takes part in the transaction process but is not the seller or buyer

mining: the process through which miners on a decentralized network add blocks to a blockchain

node: a computer on a blockchain network that stores a copy of the ledger

private key: a randomly generated number that a user of a cryptocurrency wallet needs to make transactions over the blockchain

security: a financial asset, usually in the form of a stock or bond that can be traded

smart contract: a protocol that can verify and enforce the terms of a contract without third parties

soft fork: a change to the rules of a blockchain that only invalidates old blocks

token: exchangeable digital assets that are typically based on blockchain. They can be used to pay participants for helping a blockchain function.

Source Notes

9   Martin Wolf, "The Libertarian Fantasies of Cryptocurrencies," *Financial Times*, February 3, 2019, https://medium.com/financial-times/the-libertarian -fantasies-of-cryptocurrencies-f514cc16bcd1/.

9–10   Stanton Heister and Kristi Yuthas, "The Blockchain and How It Can Influence Conceptions of the Self," *Technology in Society* 60 (February 2020), https://doi.org/10.1016/j.techsoc.2019.101218.

10   "Chancellor on Brink of Second Bailout for Banks—Satoshi's Message for Infinity," The Bitcoin News, May 24, 2018, https://thebitcoinnews.com /chancellor-on-brink-of-second-bailout-for-banks-satoshis-message-for-infinity/.

11   Nick Paumgarten, "The Prophets of Cryptocurrency Survey the Boom and Bust," *New Yorker*, October 22, 2018, https://www.newyorker.com /magazine/2018/10/22/the-prophets-of-cryptocurrency-survey-the-boom -and-bust/.

13   Xu Mingxing, Ying Tian, and Jiyue Li, *Blockchain: An Illustrated Guidebook to Understanding Blockchain*, trans. Jie Liu, (New York: Skyhorse, 2018), 9.

13, 15   Nathan Heller, "Estonia, the Digital Republic," *New Yorker*, December 11, 2017, https://www.newyorker.com/magazine/2017/12/18/estonia-the -digital-republic.

18   Omid Malekan, *The Story of Blockchain: A Beginner's Guide to the Technology That No One Understands* (Syosset, NY: Triple Smoke Stack, 2018), 16.

18   Gideon Lewis-Kraus, "Inside the Crypto World's Biggest Scandal," *Wired*, June 19, 2018, https://www.wired.com/story/tezos-blockchain-love-story -horror-story/.

18   Lewis-Kraus.

19   Marc Andreessen, "Why Bitcoin Matters," *New York Times*, January 21, 2014, https://dealbook.nytimes.com/2014/01/21/why-bitcoin-matters/.

21   Lewis-Kraus, "Inside the Crypto World's Biggest Scandal."

23–24   Nick Stockton, "A Curious Plan to Save the Environment with the Blockchain," *Wired*, May 22, 2017, https://www.wired.com/2017/05/curious-plan-save -environment-blockchain/.

25   Robyn Metcalfe, "The Life Story of Your Supermarket Chicken: Food Tracking Goes High-Tech," *Wall Street Journal*, February 21, 2019, https:// www.wsj.com/articles/the-life-story-of-your-supermarket-chicken -food-tracking-goes-high-tech-11550761202/.

26   Paumgarten, "Prophets."

26   Paumgarten.

27   Michael Casey and Paul Vigna, *The Truth Machine: The Blockchain and the Future of Everything* (New York, St. Martin's, 2018), 81–82.

27   Casey and Vigna.

31   Nellie Bowles, "Everyone Is Getting Hilariously Rich and You're Not," *New York Times*, January 13, 2018, https://www.nytimes.com/2018/01/13 /style/bitcoin-millionaires.html.

31–32   Michael Kaplan, "I Accidentally Threw Away $60 Million Worth of Bitcoin," *New York Post*, May 26, 2018, https://nypost.com/2018/05/26/i -accidentally-threw-away-60m-worth-of-bitcoin/.

33   Mark Frauenfelder, "'I Forgot My PIN': An Epic Tale of Losing $30,000 in Bitcoin," *Wired*, October 29, 2017, https://www.wired.com/story/i-forgot -my-pin-an-epic-tale-of-losing-dollar30000-in-bitcoin/.

33   Frauenfelder.

34   Sophie Haigney, "The Artist Who Guides His Art with Crypto-Tokens," *New Yorker*, September 5, 2018, https://www.newyorker.com/culture/culture -desk/the-artist-who-guides-his-art-with-crypto-tokens/.

35   Securities and Exchange Commission, July 11, 2018, https://www.sec.gov /comments/sr-cboebzx-2018-040/cboebzx2018040-167317.htm.

35   Casey and Vigna, *The Truth Machine*, 101.

35   Olga Kharif, "How's That ICO Working Out?," *Bloomberg Quint*, December 14, 2018, https://www.bloombergquint.com/businessweek/crypto-s-15 -biggest-icos-by-the-numbers/.

36   Wolf, "Libertarian Fantasies."

36   Lionel Laurent, "Decentralized Elites," *Bloomberg Businessweek*, December 14, 2018, https://www.scribd.com/article/395641199/Decentralized-Elites/.

40   Paul Krugman, "Transaction Costs and Tethers: Why I'm a Crypto Skeptic," *New York Times*, July 31, 2018, https://www.nytimes.com/2018/07/31 /opinion/transaction-costs-and-tethers-why-im-a-crypto-skeptic.html.

41   Dan McCrum, "Sell All Crypto and Abandon All Blockchain," *Financial Times*, April 13, 2018, https://ftalphaville.ft.com/2018/04/13/1523592006000 /Sell-all-crypto-and-abandon-all-blockchain/.

41   Tae Kim, "Warren Buffett Says Bitcoin Is 'Probably Rat Poison Squared,'" CNBC, May 5, 2018, https://www.cnbc.com/2018/05/05/warren -buffett-says-bitcoin-is-probably-rat-poison-squared.html.

41–42   George Gilder, *Life after Google* (Washington, DC: Regnery Gateway, 2018), 126.

42   Laurent, "Decentralized Elites."

43   Nellie Bowles, "Remember Bitcoin? Some Investors Might Want to Forget," *New York Times*, December 27, 2018, https://www.nytimes.com/2018/12 /27/technology/bitcoin-cryptocurrency-crash.html.

43   Izabella Kaminska, "From the HODL to a Crypto Winter," *Financial Times*, February 26, 2019, https://ftalphaville.ft.com/2019/02/26 /1551157202000/From-the-HODL-to-a-crypto-winter/.

43   Alexandra Stevenson and Su-Hyun Lee, "Cryptocurrency Was Their Way Out of South Korea's Lowest Rungs," *New York Times*, February 11, 2019, https://www.nytimes.com/2019/02/10/business/south-korea-bitcoin -cryptocurrencies.html.

44 Camilla Hodgson, "Crypto Currency Founder Revealed as Winner of Buffett Lunch," *Financial Times*, June 4, 2019, https://www.ft.com/content /ac6db9f0-8624-11e9-97ea-05ac2431f453/.

45 Gary Shilling, "Scoreboard," Forbes 151, no. 4 (February 15, 1993): 236.

45 Bowles, "Remember Bitcoin?"

45 Bowles.

45 Jemima Kelly, "A Failed ICO Is Trying to Flog Itself on eBay," *Financial Times*, March 25, 2019, https://ftalphaville.ft.com/2019/03/25 /1553498702000/A-failed-ICO-is-trying-to-flog-itself-on-eBay-/.

45 Kelly.

46 GameKyuubi, "I AM HODLING," bitcointalk.org, accessed March 31, 2020, https://bitcointalk.org/index.php?topic=375643.0.

46 Tracy Alloway, "After the Crazy, the Reality," *Bloomberg Businessweek*, December 14, 2018, https://www.scribd.com/article/395641179/After -The-Crazy-The-Reality/.

47 Bowles, "Everyone."

50 Robert McMillan, "The Inside Story of Mt. Gox, Bitcoin's $460 Million Disaster," *Wired*, March 3, 2014, https://www.wired.com/2014/03 /bitcoin-exchange/.

51 Justin Scheck and Bradley Hope, "The Man Who Solved Bitcoin's Most Notorious Heist," *Wall Street Journal*, August 10, 2018, https://www.wsj .com/articles/the-man-who-solved-bitcoins-most-notorious-heist-1533917805/.

51 Jack Stubbs, Karolina Tagaris, and Anna Irrera, "US Indicts Suspected Russian 'Mastermind' of $4 Billion Bitcoin Laundering Scheme," Reuters, July 26, 2017, https://www.reuters.com/article/US-greece-russia-arrest -idUSKBN1AB1OP/.

54 Matthew Leising, "The Ether Thief," Bloomberg, June 13, 2017, https:// www.bloomberg.com/features/2017-the-ether-thief/.

54 Mike Orcutt, "Once Hailed as Unhackable, Blockchains Are Now Getting Hacked," *MIT Technology Review*, February 19, 2019, https://www. technologyreview.com/s/612974/once-hailed-as-unhackable-blockchains- are-now-getting-hacked/.

55 Leising, "The Ether Thief."

55 Gilder, *Life after Google*, 154.

57 Paul Vigna and Shane Shifflett, "'Our Cash Went to Something:' Customers Hunt for Bankrupt Crypto Exchange's Missing Millions," *Wall Street Journal*, February 19, 2019, https://www.wsj.com/articles/our-cash-went-to -something-customers-hunt-for-bankrupt-crypto-exchanges-missing-millions -11550596908/.

58 Bruce Schneier, "There's No Good Reason to Trust Blockchain Technology," *Wired*, February 6, 2019, https://www.wired.com/story /theres-no-good -reason-to-trust-blockchain-technology/.

58 Noah Smith, "Blockchain Hype Missed the Mark, and Not by a Little," Bloomberg, May 3, 2019, https://www.bloomberg.com/opinion /articles/2019-05-03/blockchain-hype-missed-the-mark-and-not-by-a -little/.

58 Kai Stinchcombe, "Blockchain Is Not Only Crappy Technology but a Bad Vision for the Future," Medium, April 5, 2018, https://medium.com/@ kaistinchcombe/decentralized-and-trustless-crypto-paradise-is-actually-a -medieval-hellhole-c1ca122efdec/.

59 Stinchcombe.

59 Stinchcombe.

59 Stinchcombe.

59–60 Stinchcombe.

60 McCrum, "Sell All Crypto."

61 Paul Vigna, "CryptoKitties and Dice Games Fail to Lure Users to Dapps," Wall Street Journal, May 29, 2019, https://www.wsj.com/articles /cryptokitties-and-dice-games-fail-to-lure-users-to-dapps-11559122201/.

63 Nathanial Popper, "After the Bust, Are Bitcoins More Like Tulip Mania or the Internet?," New York Times, April 23, 2019, https://www.nytimes.com/2019 /04/23/technology/bitcoin-tulip-mania-internet.html.

65 Gilder, Life after Google, 153.

68 Stockton, "A Curious Plan."

68 Casey and Vigna, The Truth Machine, 181.

69 Gilder, Life after Google, 126.

69 Fred Imbert, "JPMorgan CEO Jamie Dimon Says Bitcoin Is a 'Fraud' That Will Eventually Blow Up," CNBC, September 12, 2017, https://www.cnbc .com/2017/09/12/jpmorgan-ceo-jamie-dimon-raises-flag-on-trading- revenue-sees-20-percent-fall-for-the-third-quarter.html.

70 Michael J. de la Merced and Nathaniel Popper, "JPMorgan Chase Tests Own Cryptocurrency, the First for a US Bank," New York Times, February 14, 2019, https://www.nytimes.com/2019/02/14/business/dealbook /jpmorgan-cryptocurrency-bitcoin.html.

71 Alastair Marsh and Silla Brush, "Why Crypto Companies Still Can't Open Checking Accounts," Bloomberg, March 3, 2019, https://www.bloomberg .com/news/articles/2019-03-03/why-crypto-companies-still-can-t-open -checking-accounts/.

76 Ludwig Siegele, "How to Fix What Has Gone Wrong with the Internet," Economist, July 3, 2018, https://medium.com/@the_economist/how-to -fix-what-has-gone-wrong-with-the-internet-3ffc51419a40/.

76–77 Casey and Vigna, The Truth Machine, 115.

77 Mike Isaac, Nathaniel Popper, and Cecilia Kang, "PayPal Pulls Out of Libra, Facebook's Cryptocurrency Project," New York Times, October 4, 2019,

https://www.nytimes.com/2019/10/04/technology/paypal-facebook
-cryptocurrency-libra.html.

77–78 Ryan Browne, "Libra Shows Facebook Is Financially 'Tone-Deaf,' CNET Founder Says," CNBC, November 6, 2019, https://www.cnbc.com/2019 /11/06/web-summit-cnet-founder-says-facebooks-libra-is-tone-deaf.html.

78 Ben Fox Rubin, "Congress Pillories Zuckerberg over Libra Cryptocurrency," CNET, October 23, 2019, https://www.cnet.com/news/congress-pillories -zuckerberg-over-libra-cryptocurrency/.

78–79 Kiran Stacey and Hannah Murphy, "Zuckerberg Admits Facebook in a Poor Position to Promote Libra," *Financial Times*, October 22, 2019, https:// www.ft.com/content/b582c76a-f4f1-11e9-b018-3ef8794b17c6/.

79 "Blockchain Frenzy That Xi Started Gets Warning from China Media," Bloomberg News, October 28, 2019, https://www.bloomberg.com /news/articles/2019-10-29/china-s-state-media-warns-on-blockchain -frenzy-that-xi-started/.

80 Kashmir Hill, "Bitcoin Creator Returns To Internet To Say, 'I Am Not Dorian Nakamoto,'" Forbes, March 6, 2014, https://www.forbes.com/sites/ kashmirhill/2014/03/06/bitcoin-creator-returns-to-internet-to-say-i-am-not- dorian-nakamoto/#6504d0c476bb/.

80 Andy Greenberg, "New Clues Suggest Craig Wright, Suspected Bitcoin Creator, May Be a Hoaxer," *Wired*, December 11, 2015, https:// www.wired.com/2015/12/new-clues-suggest-satoshi-suspect-craig -wright-may-be-a-hoaxer/.

81 Laurence Fletcher and Hudson Lockett, "Bitcoin Rises Again as Analysts Declare End of 'Crypto Winter,'" *Financial Times*, May 27, 2019, https:// www.ft.com/content/daec39ce-8092-11e9-9935-ad75bb96c849/.

82 Mike Orcutt, "In 2019, Blockchain Will Start to Become Boring," *MIT Technology Review*, January 2, 2019, https://www.technologyreview .com/s/612687/in-2019-blockchains-will-start-to-become-boring/.

82 Orcutt.

83 "The Future of Money in the Digital Age," Peterson Institute for International Economics, streamed live October 16, 2019, YouTube video, 2:39:26, https://www.youtube.com/watch?v=RCZxEx7RbkM/.

83 Martin Wolf, "The Threat and the Promise of Digital Money," *Financial Times*, October 22, 2019, https://www.ft.com/content/fc079a6a-f4ad-11e9 -a79c-bc9acae3b654/.

Further Information

Day, Mark Stuart. *Bits to Bitcoin: How Our Digital Stuff Works.* Cambridge, MA: MIT Press, 2018. This book describes the digital infrastructure (software) beneath our operating systems and explains how blockchain allows different parties to trust one another.

Gilder, George. *Life after Google: The Fall of Big Data and the Rise of the Blockchain Economy.* Washington, DC: Regnery Gateway, 2018. A far-reaching description of the tech world today as dominated by Google, and why blockchain will replace it.

Lewis, Antony. *The Basics of Bitcoins and Blockchains: An Introduction to Cryptocurrencies and the Technology That Powers Them.* Coral Gables, FL: Mango, 2018. As the title implies, this is a no-nonsense introduction to cryptocurrencies and the blockchain technology that allows them to function.

Malekan, Omid. *The Story of the Blockchain: A Beginner's Guide to the Technology Nobody Understands.* Syosset, NY: Triple Smoke Stack, 2018. This book explains in very simple terms how cryptocurrencies were created, how they have evolved, and the crises they have faced throughout their short history.

Tapscott, Don, and Alex Tapscott. *Blockchain Revolution: How the Technology behind Bitcoin Is Changing Money, Business, and the World.* New York: Penguin, 2016. Read about the implications of Bitcoin and blockchain technology in all aspects of the economy and society.

Vigna, Paul, and Michael J. Casey. *The Truth Machine: The Blockchain and the Future of Everything.* New York: St. Martin's, 2018. This is an in-depth exploration of blockchain and how it enables strangers to enter into agreements without an intermediary.

Index

About the Author

Brendan January has been a financial writer on Wall Street for more than a decade and is an award-winning author of more than twenty nonfiction books for young readers. Some of his most recent titles include *Information Insecurity: Privacy under Siege* and *ISIS: The Global Face of Terrorism*. January attended Haverford College in Pennsylvania and the Columbia Graduate School of Journalism in New York. He was also a Fulbright scholar in Germany. He lives with his wife and two children in Maplewood, New Jersey.

Acknowledgments

Image credits: Suriyapong Koktong/EyeEm/Getty Images, p. 6; Patrick Foto/Getty Images, p. 9; TommL/Getty Images, p. 11; OLGA MALTSEVA/AFP/Getty Images, p. 16; John Phillips/TechCrunch/Getty Images, p. 26; Artur Widak/NurPhoto/Getty Images, p. 31; © CryptoKitties, p. 33; PHILIPPE LOPEZ/AFP/Getty Images, p. 41; Ja'Crispy/Shutterstock.com, p. 42; Daniel Zuchnik/WireImage/Getty Images, p. 44; QUENTIN TYBERGHIEN/AFP/Getty Images, p. 49; Nes/Getty Images, p. 50; Nicolas Economou/NurPhoto/Getty Images, p. 52; Aha-Soft/Shutterstock.com, p. 57; Bumble Dee/Shutterstock.com, p. 69; Timon Stalder/EyeEm/Getty Images, p. 73; JOSH EDELSON/AFP/Getty Images, p. 78; Paras Griffin/OWN/Getty Images, p. 81; Tetra Images/Getty Images, p. 82.
Design elements: filo/Getty Images.
Cover image: filo/Getty Images.